I0789778

preface

I've lived in the East Village for over 30 years and like most who live or travel into this unique and eclectic neighborhood, there is one constant... you never know what you're going to hear or see on the streets or in some local bar. The East Village houses a variety of classic characters who express themselves freely on topics from music and art to business and exploding tattoos. This book was compiled mainly while I would sit and sketch at my local St. Mark's bar, Bull McCabes. The quotes come from actual conversations or overheard lines that I've experienced while sipping a cold beer, enjoying a game, or sitting outside and watching the constant flow of people between 2nd and 3rd Avenue, or what I like to call St. Marks TV [thanks Buddy]. I'd like to thank all those whose quotes have made life in the East Village a rare and enjoyable place and to all the bartenders who served drinks to those people. Thanks for helping open up their minds and mouths and making it easier for them to spit out a classic quote.

BILLY THE ARTIST

Some readers may find parts of this book offensive or triggering. The following book in no way represents the opinions, beliefs, or statements of the press, its staff, volunteers, or the author of this book. The following statements are taken directly from bar conversations as heard by the artist and are intended to be sociological by offering an unflinching look at bar-culture talk as noted by the artist. The press believes in the equality of all people regardless of gender, ethnicity, religion, race, or creed.

All Rights Reserved

Published in the United States of America

First Edition
1 2 3 4 5 6 7 8 9

Selections of up to two pages may be reproduced without permission. To reproduce more than two pages of any one portion of this book write to C&R Press publishers John Gosslee and Andrew H. Sullivan.

Copyright ©2020 Billy The Artist

ISBN - 978-1-949540-17-8

C&R Press
Conscious & Responsible
crpress.org
Long Live Books!

For special discounted bulk purchases, please contact:
C&R Press sales@crpress.org
Contact info@crpress.org to book events, readings and author signings.

Printed in United States

THINGS
YOU DON'T HEAR TWICE:
QUOTES FROM THE EAST VILLAGE, NYC

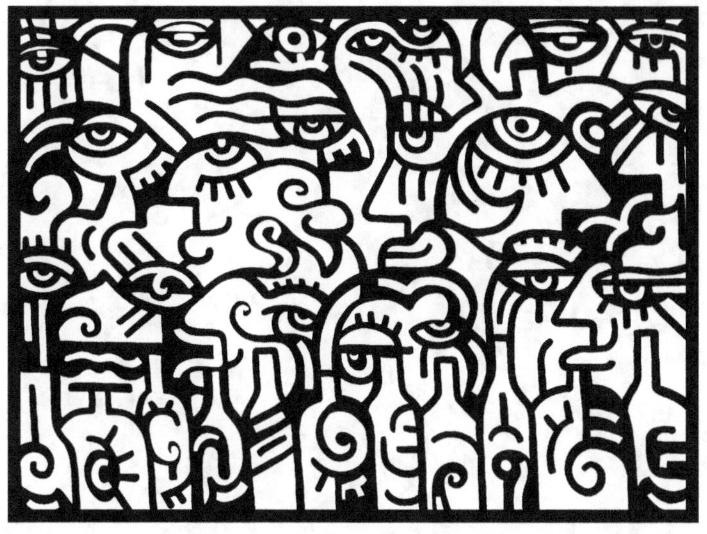

DRAWINGS AND QUOTES COMPILED BY
BILLY THE ARTIST

bar life

Why don't you get pregnant the way I did?
Because I don't like vodka, mother.

Mother & daughter

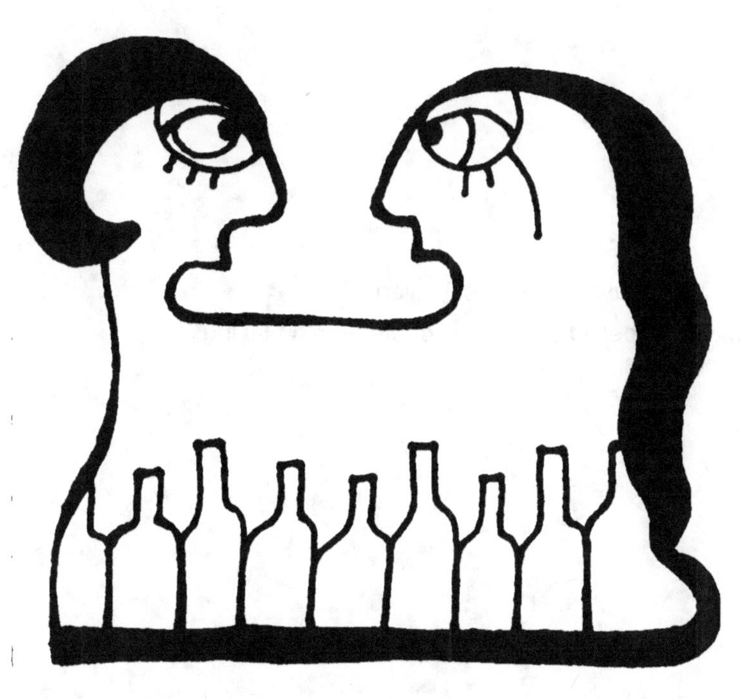

Hey Mike, have you ever skydived.

No, but I repelled out of a helicopter into a blazing fire of chaos.

Vietnam Mike

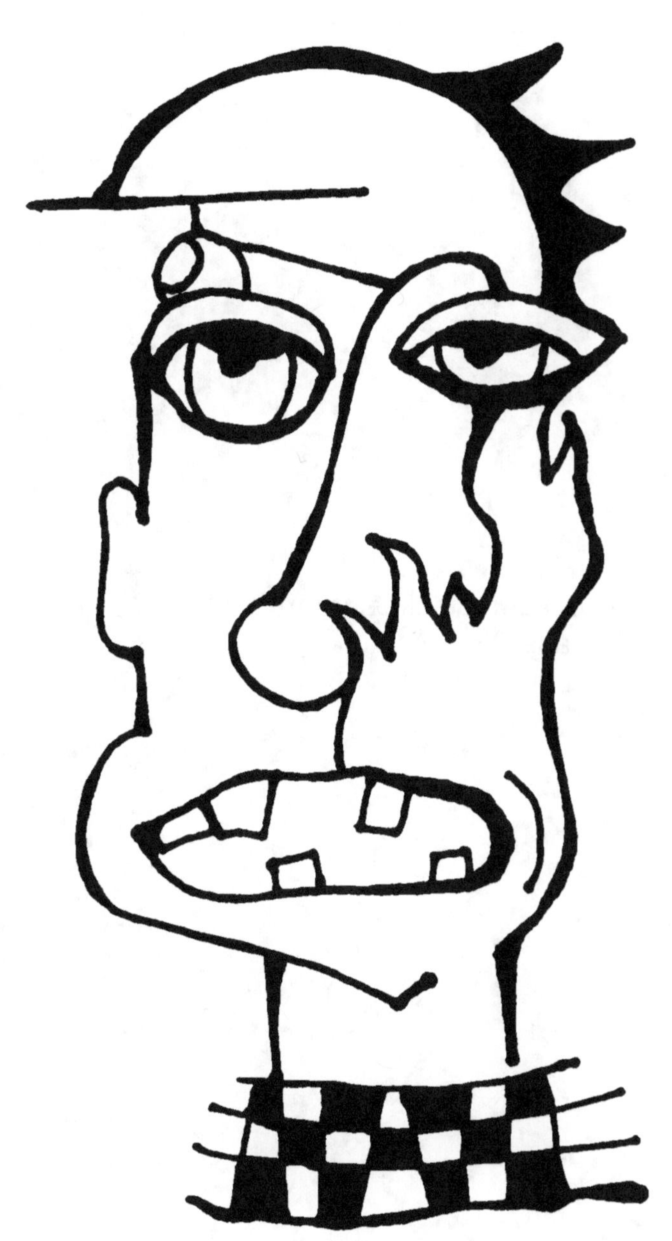

She had so much plastic surgery... when she
smiled her ass lifted up.

Angry James

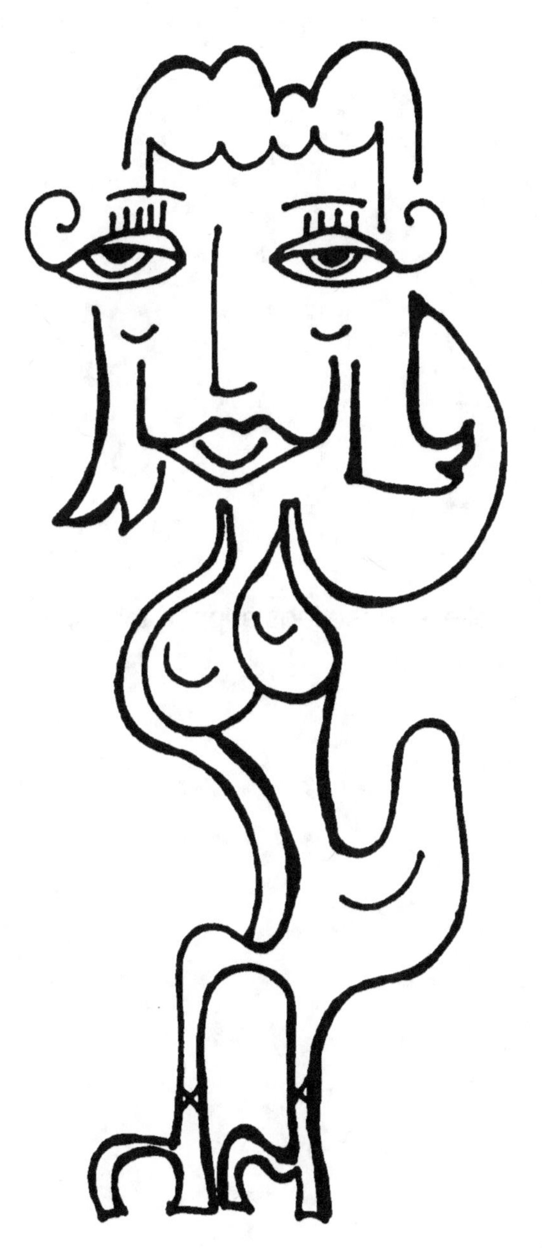

It's hard to believe those legs support that ass.

MCJ

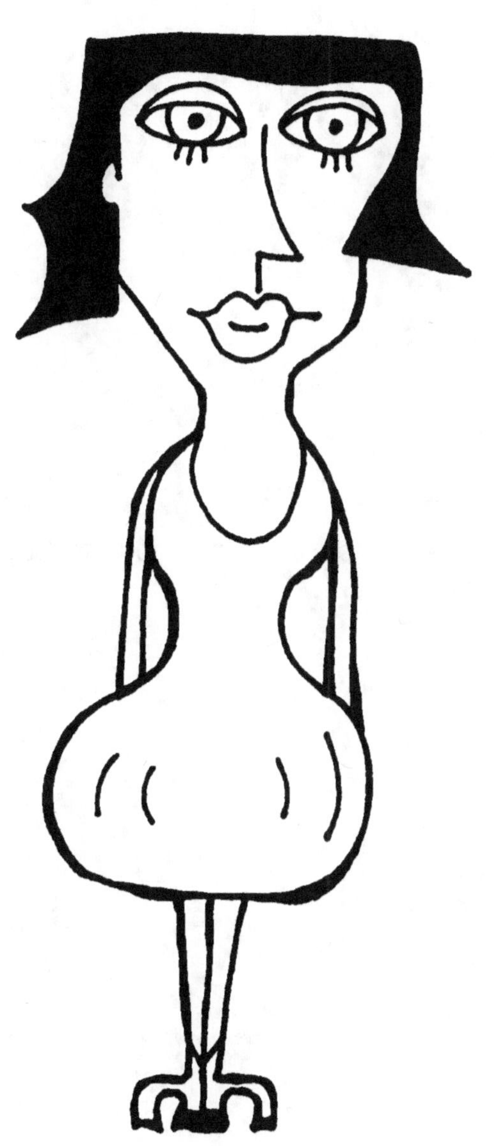

Bang Mrs. Howell a few times and you can buy
Maryanne and Ginger.

TV Mike

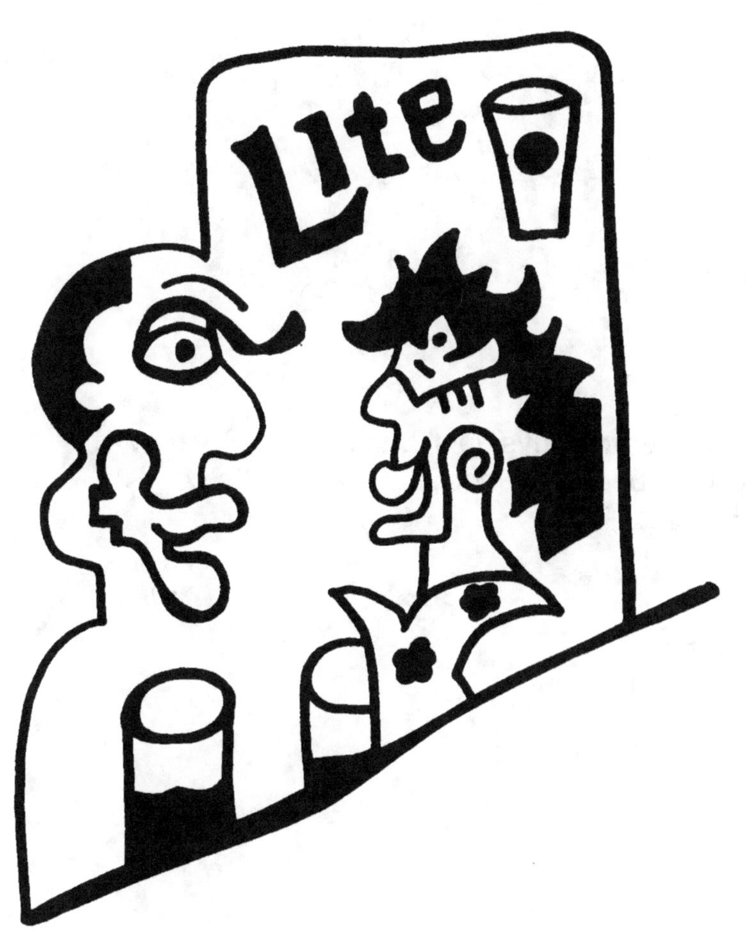
Lite

So, how you guys doin'?... Good?... So, how you've been?... Good?... Okay, I gotta go.

Glen the Mailman

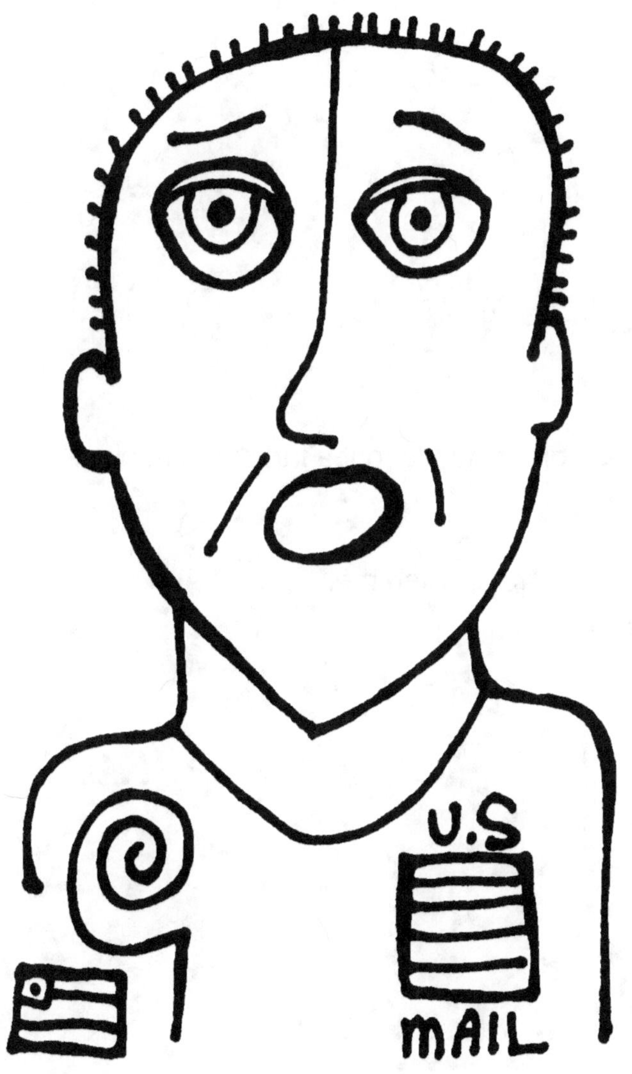

U.S
MAIL

I've got a great story about a fart and a hooker.

Angry James

That hooker really liked me.

Anonymous

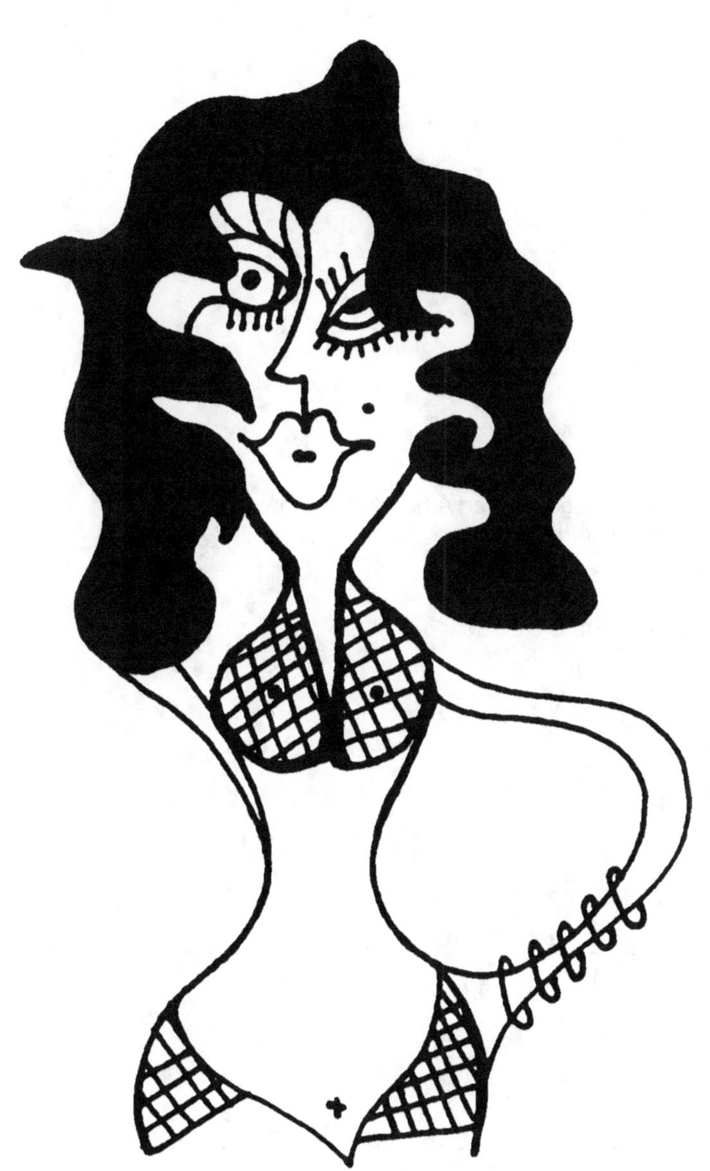

I told you I met a girl named Amanda Swallows...
no, I checked her I.D.

Buddy the Bouncer

Hey, I'm Amanda Swallows.

Amanda Swallows

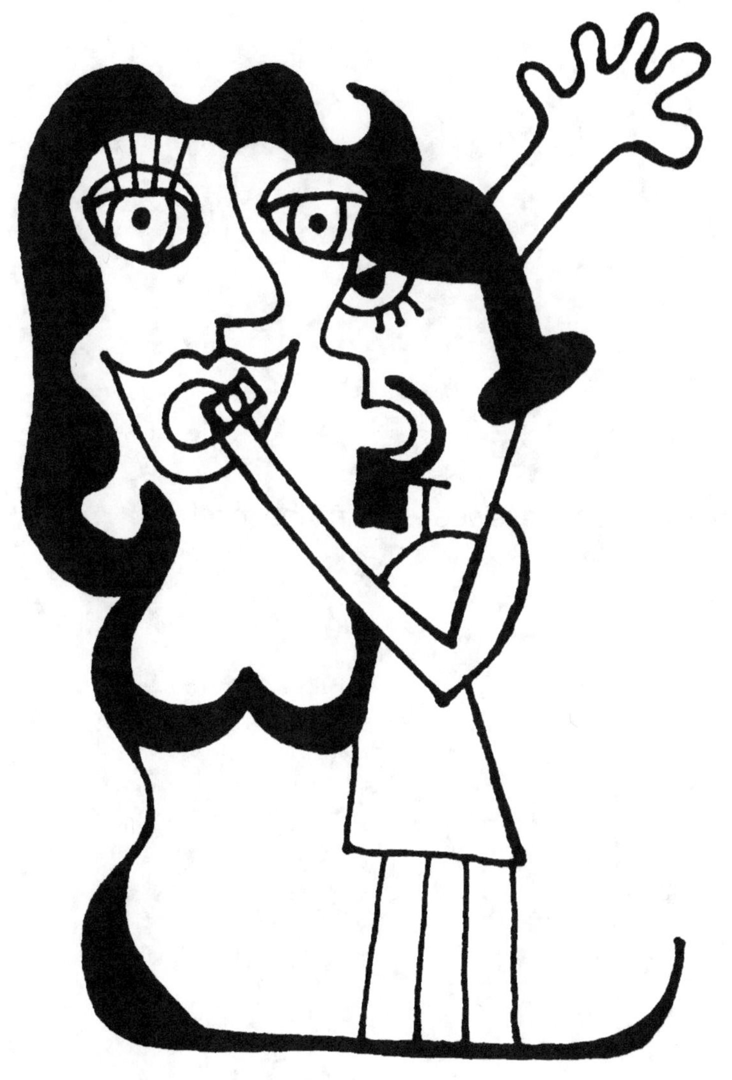

That's <u>me</u> smellin sweet... it ain't the roses.

Guy who sells roses

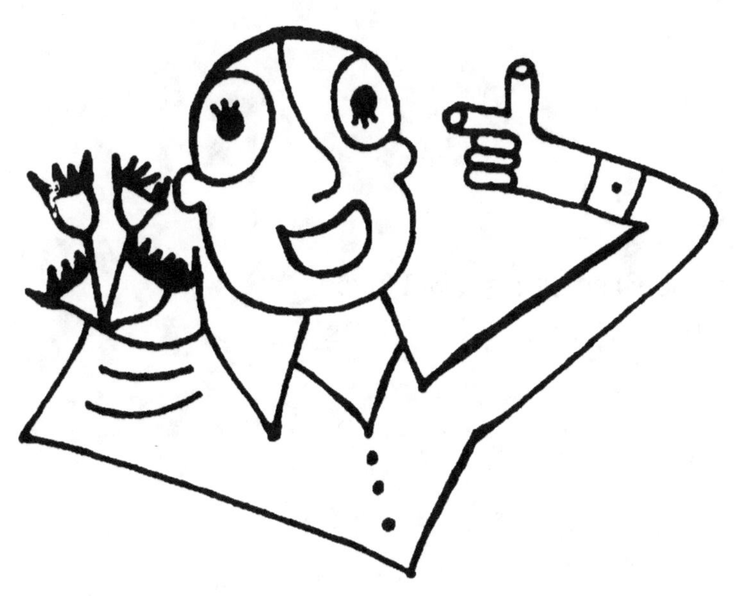

And now I smell like a wet futton.

Benwuzhear

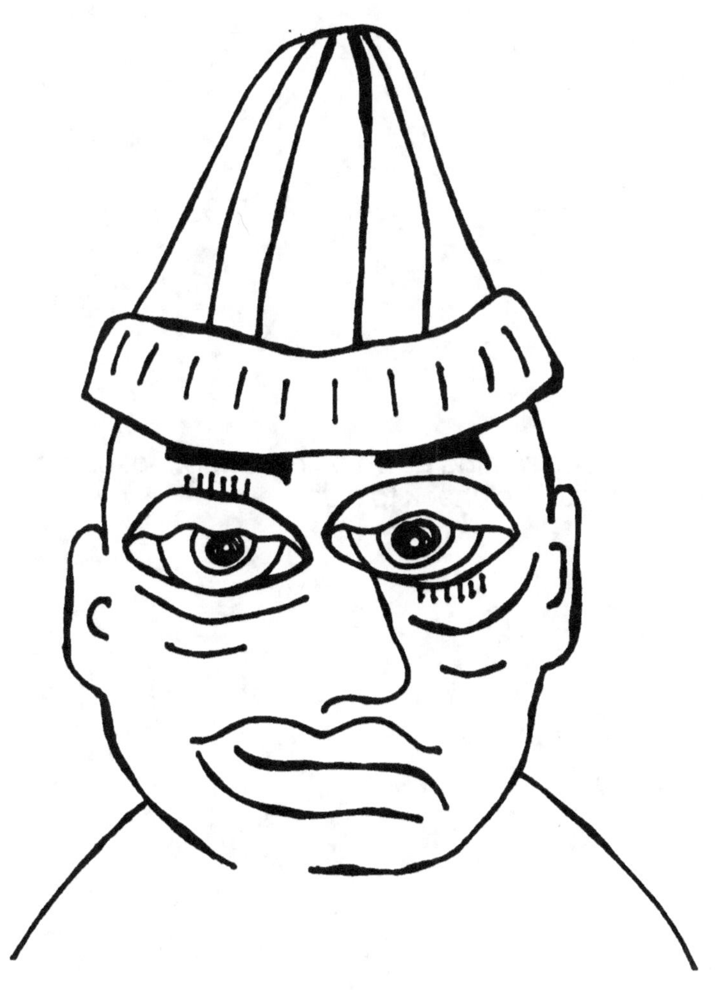

Money's been raining down on me lately... of course I'm waiting for the check to clear.

BTA

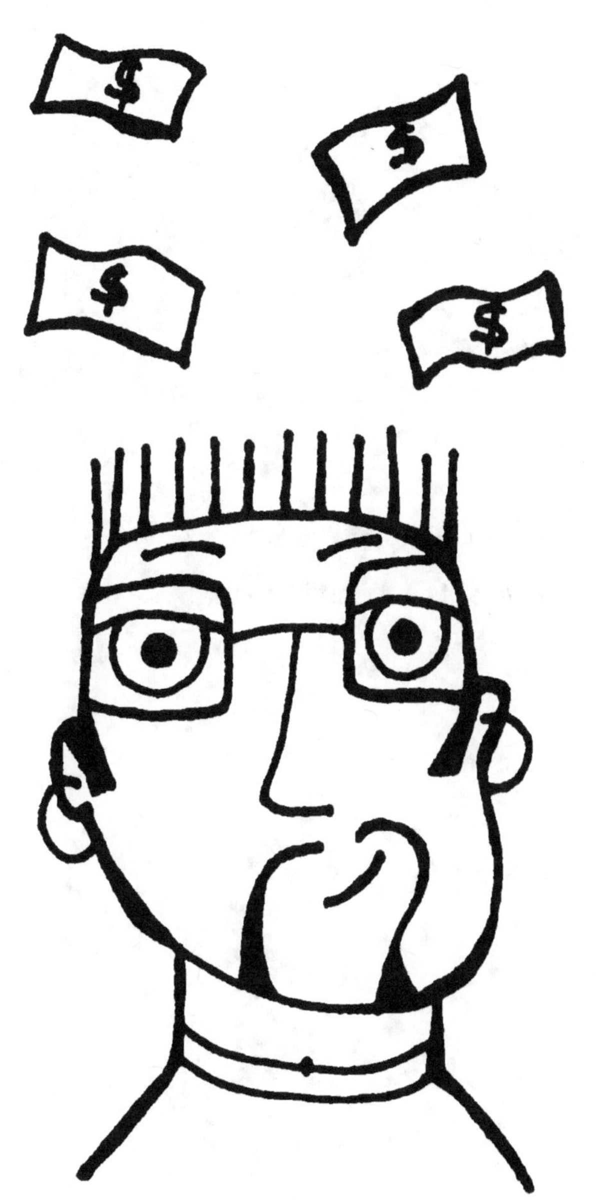

I <u>am</u> a guy with tits... I don't like that.

Stoner

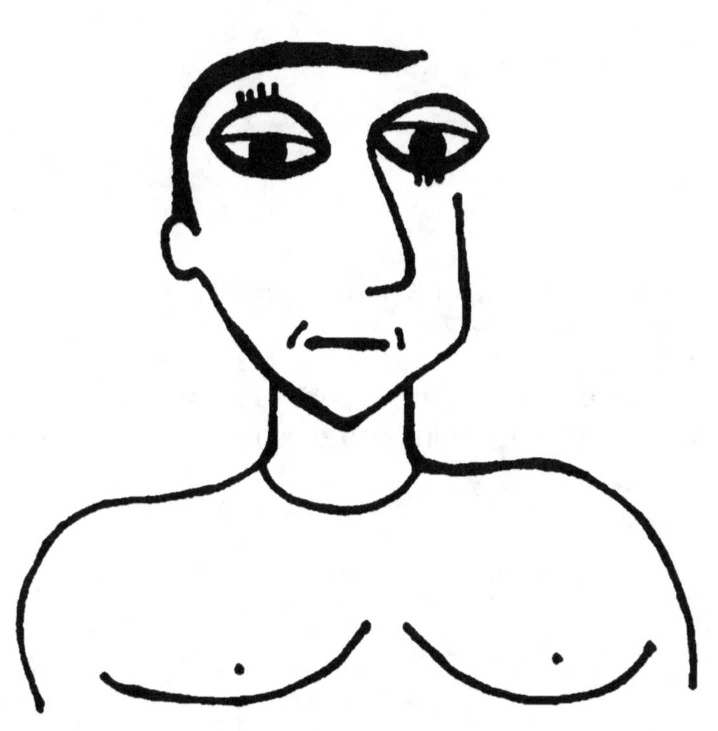

Hey, I have an idea for a porno... Mary Kate takes it in the Ashley.

Here's another one... the Michael Jackson penalty... illegal touching of the ball.

Motor Sheckey James

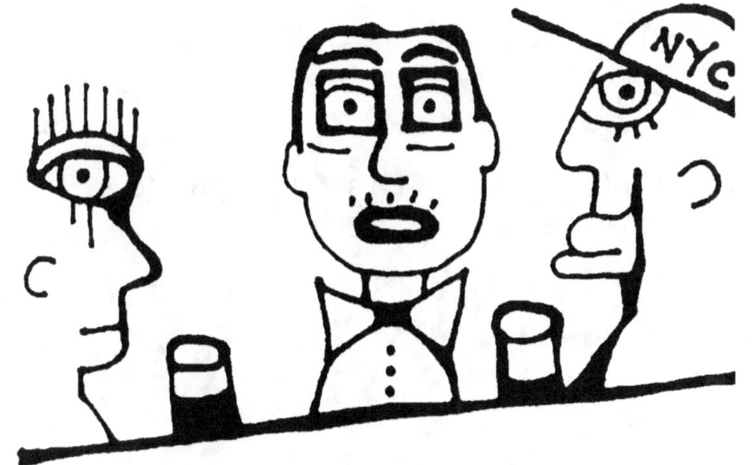

NYC

I don't want a bartender with shtick... I want to beat them to death.

M

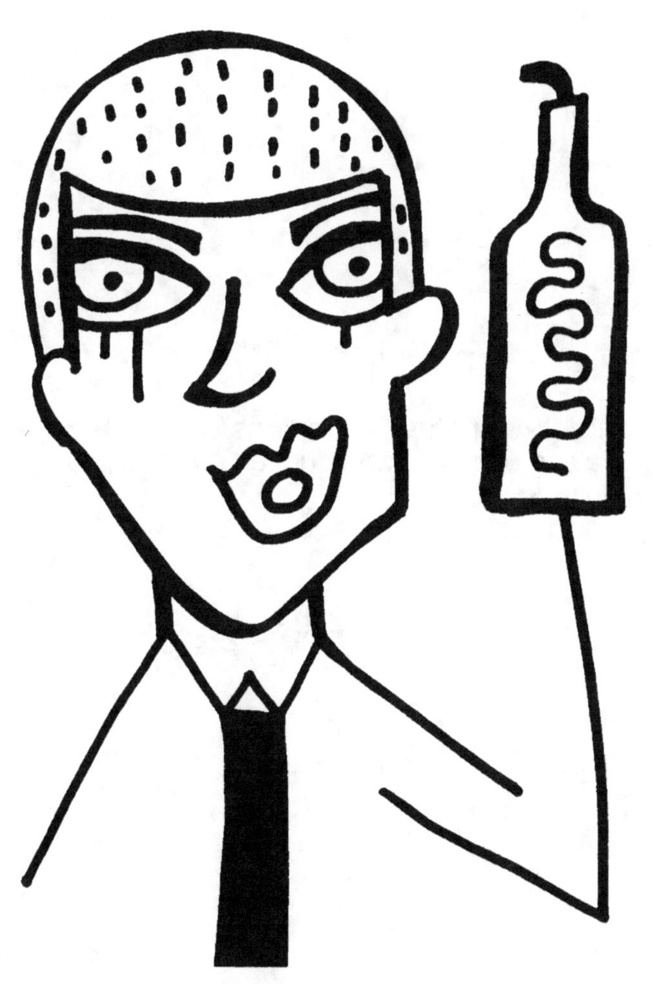

The song, "We are the Champions".... it's about queers taking over the world, united under a pink banner with a boner on it.

Mike Rock

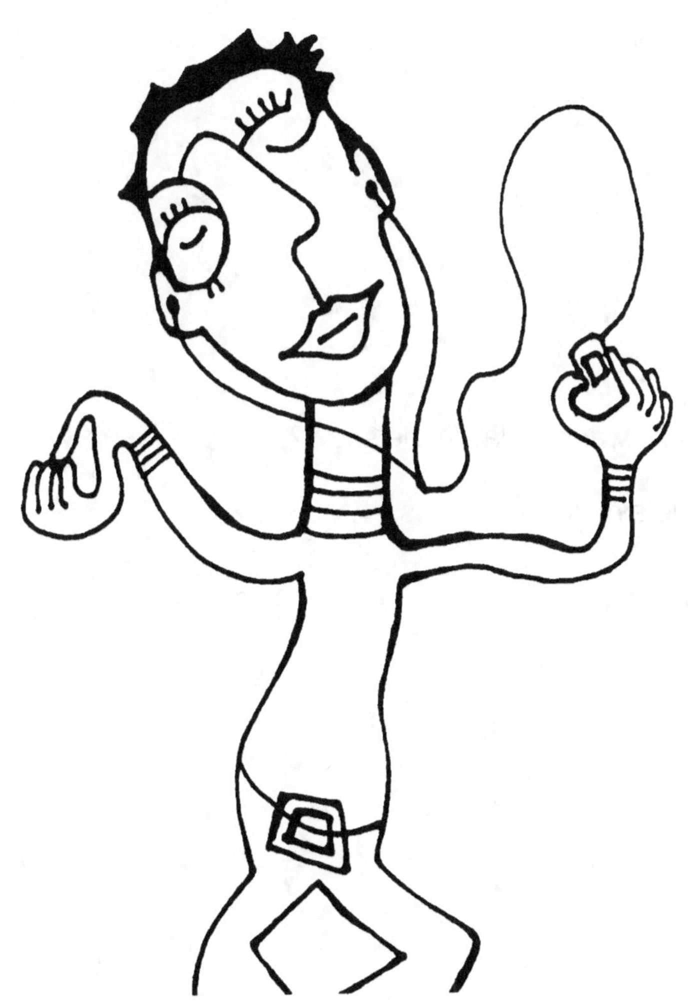

Do you want to play in the snow?

No, lets make jizz babies.

Jay

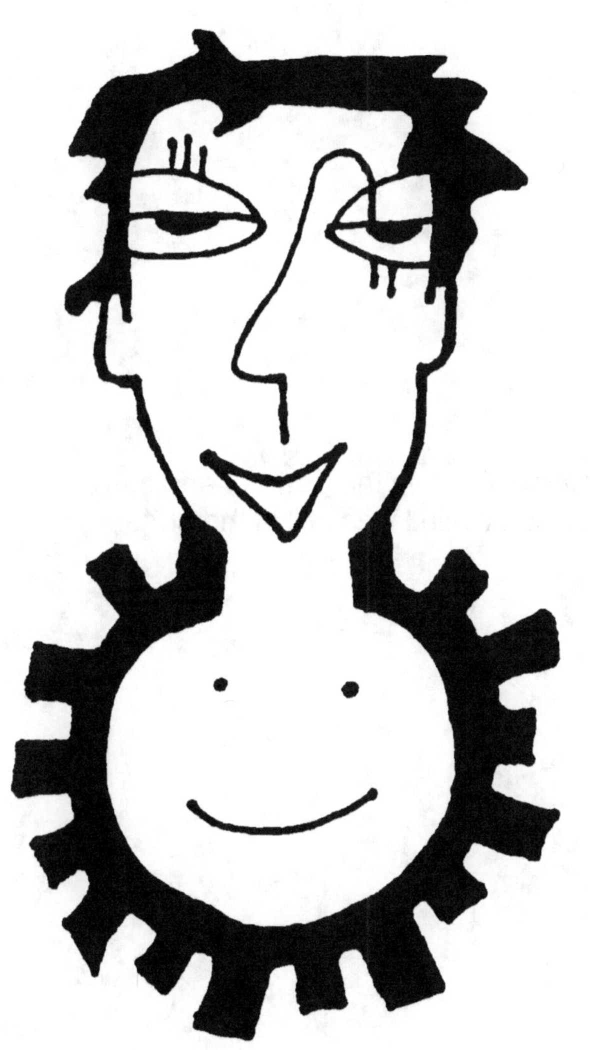

I actually woke up in the gutter... and then hailed a cab while I was still _in_ the gutter.

Freeze

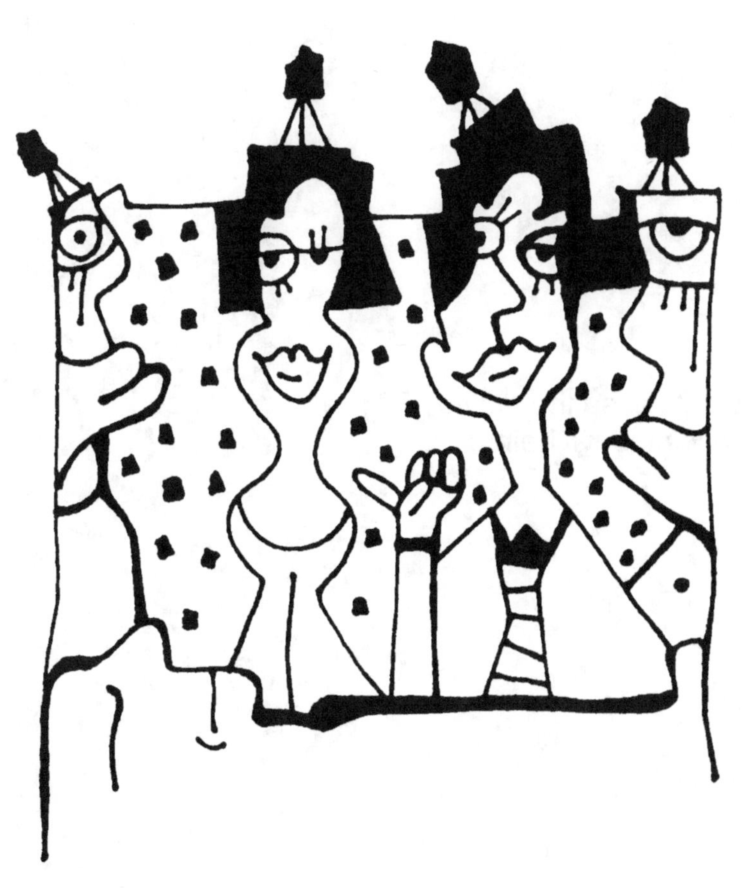

I went to see the movie "Elf"... you don't need
the joint, but it helps.

ETB

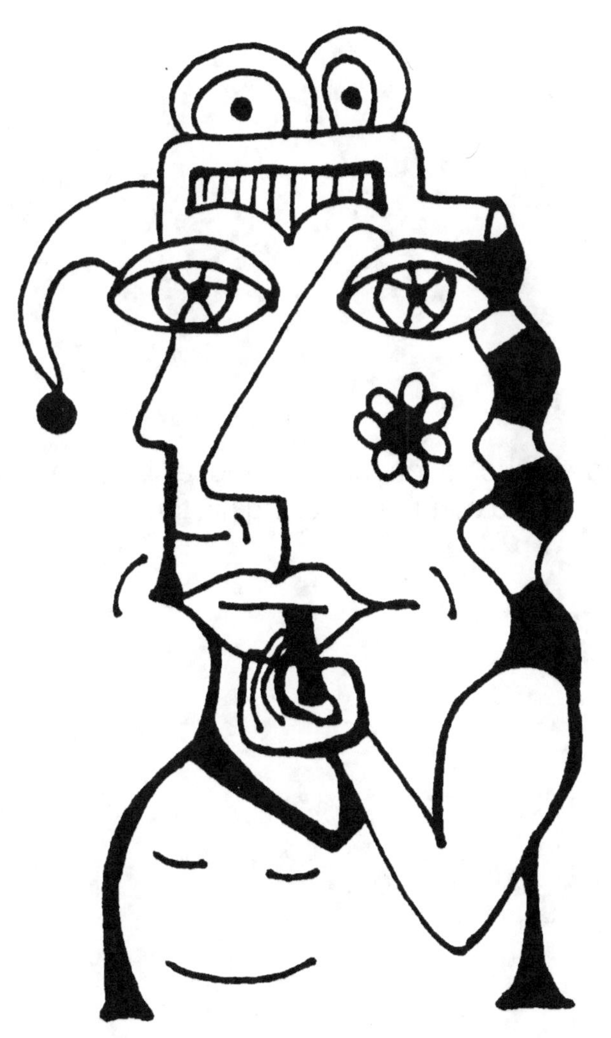

This guy is such a loser... he could fall into a bag of nipples and come up sucking his thumb.

Decklin

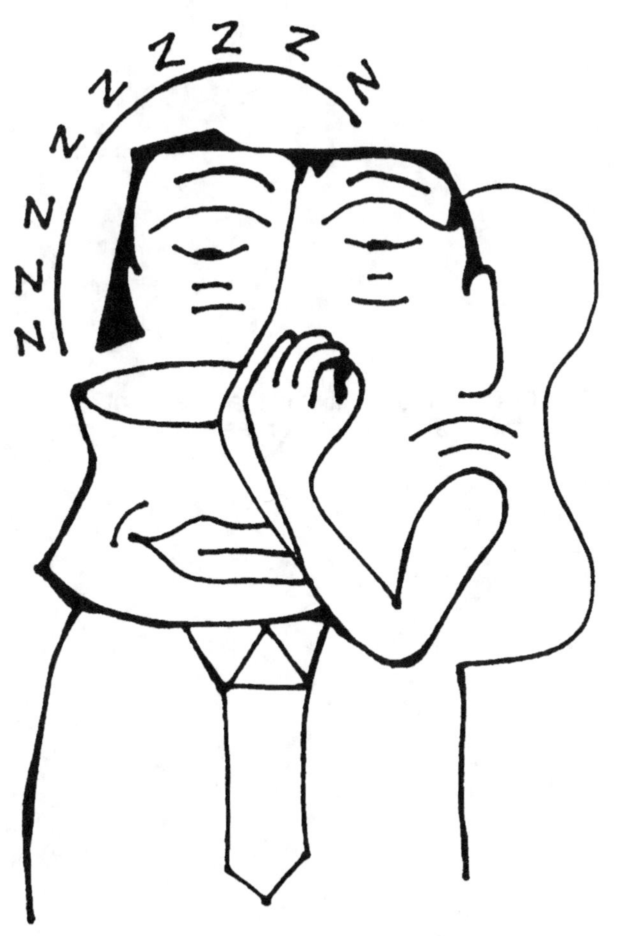

She smelled like a stripper... it was that pleasant
mixture of patchouli and chicken grease.

Motor

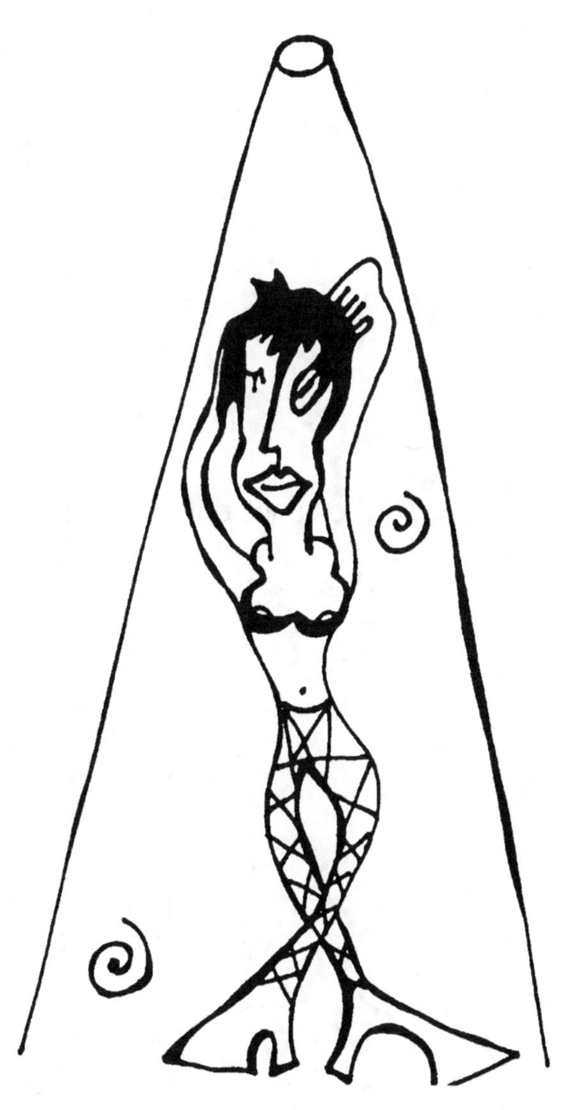

I'm the weird old guy who hangs out at parties with sorority girls.

McCloud

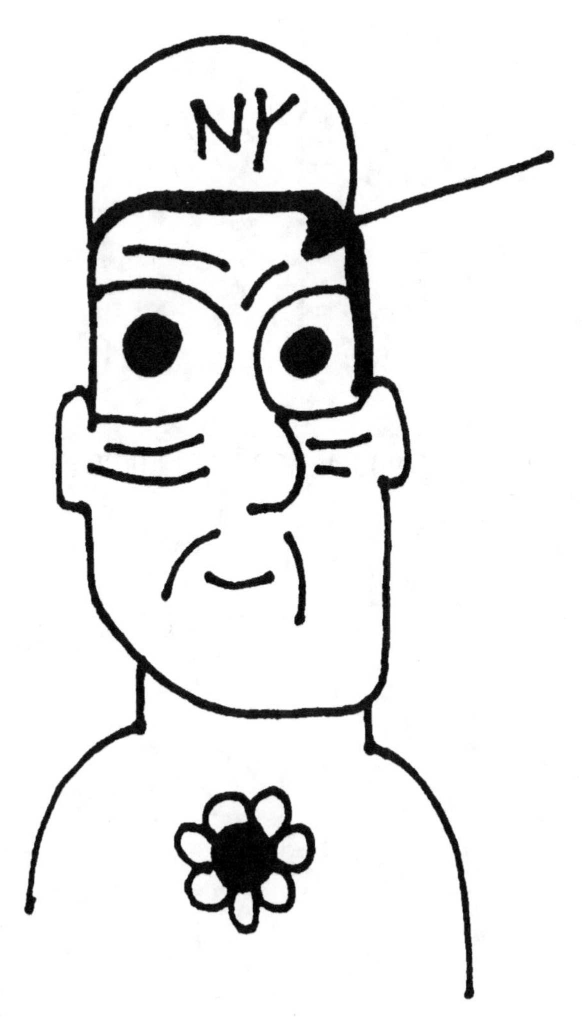

NY

Fellas... you're looking at a serial momma in that baby basket.

Tommy

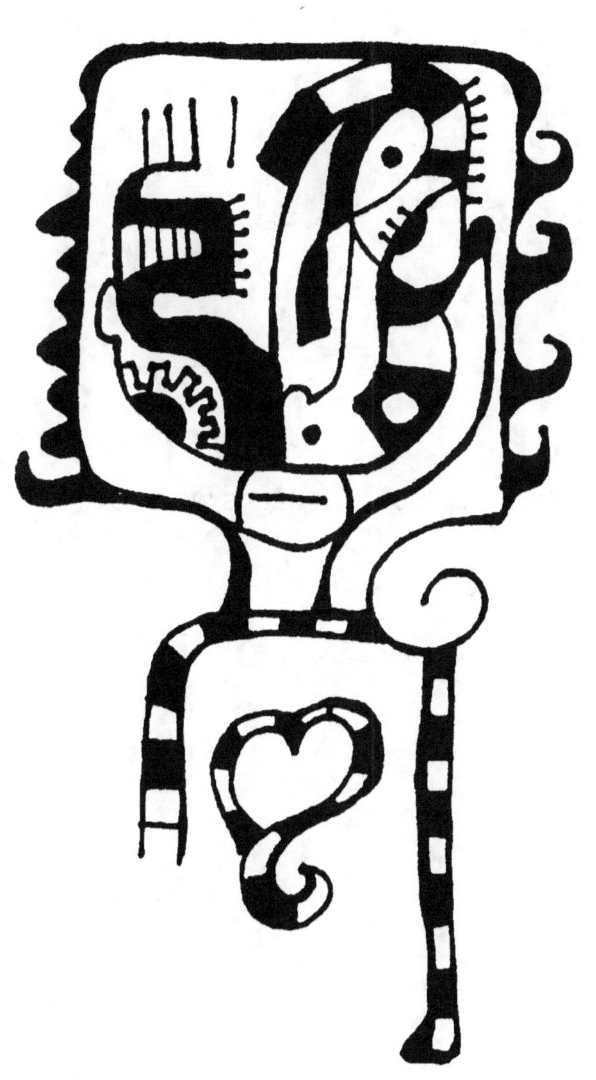

If we threw out all the crack heads we'd have no
business.

Erica the Bartender

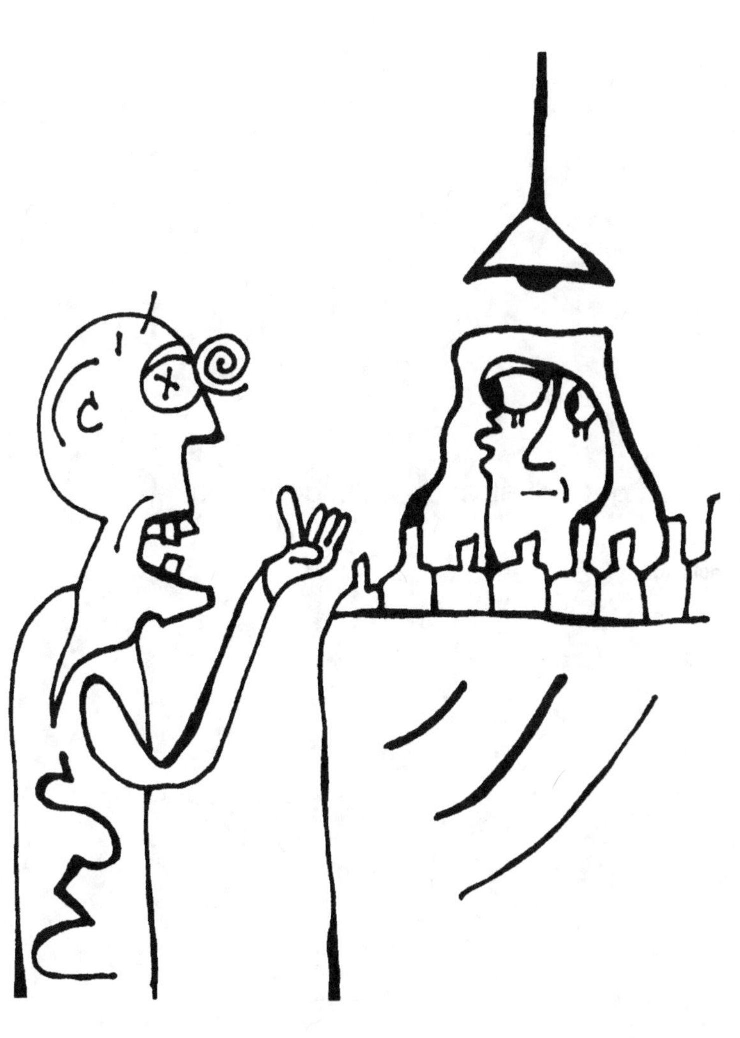

If I don't get a drink soon... I'm gonna puke.

Budstock

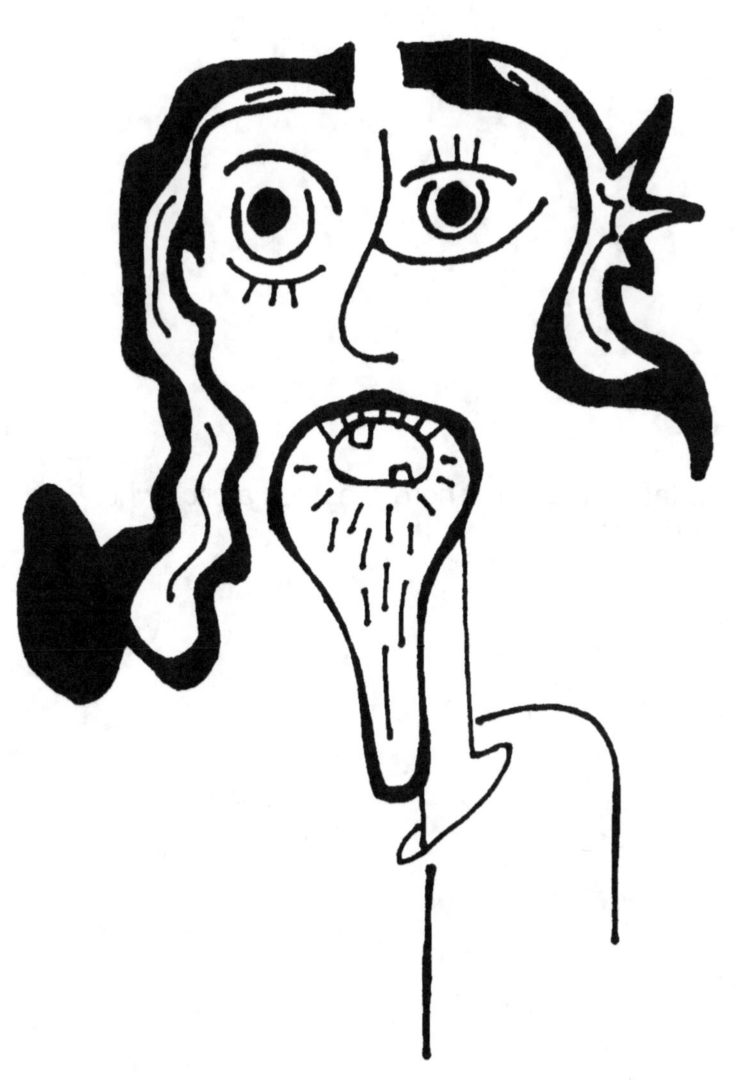

Now that Buddy's not here, we need a bitch who
knows it all.

MCJ

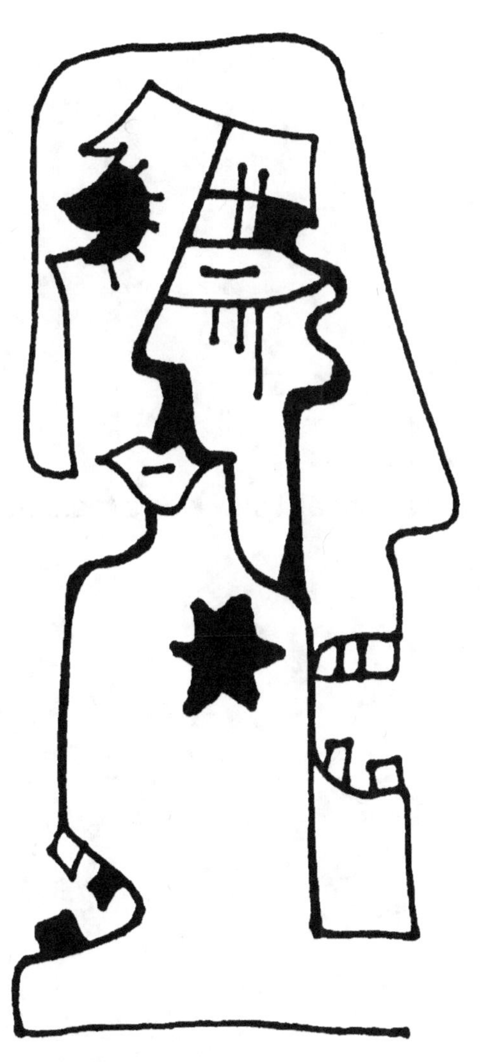

When I looked at him all I saw was a toe... no camel.

Suke

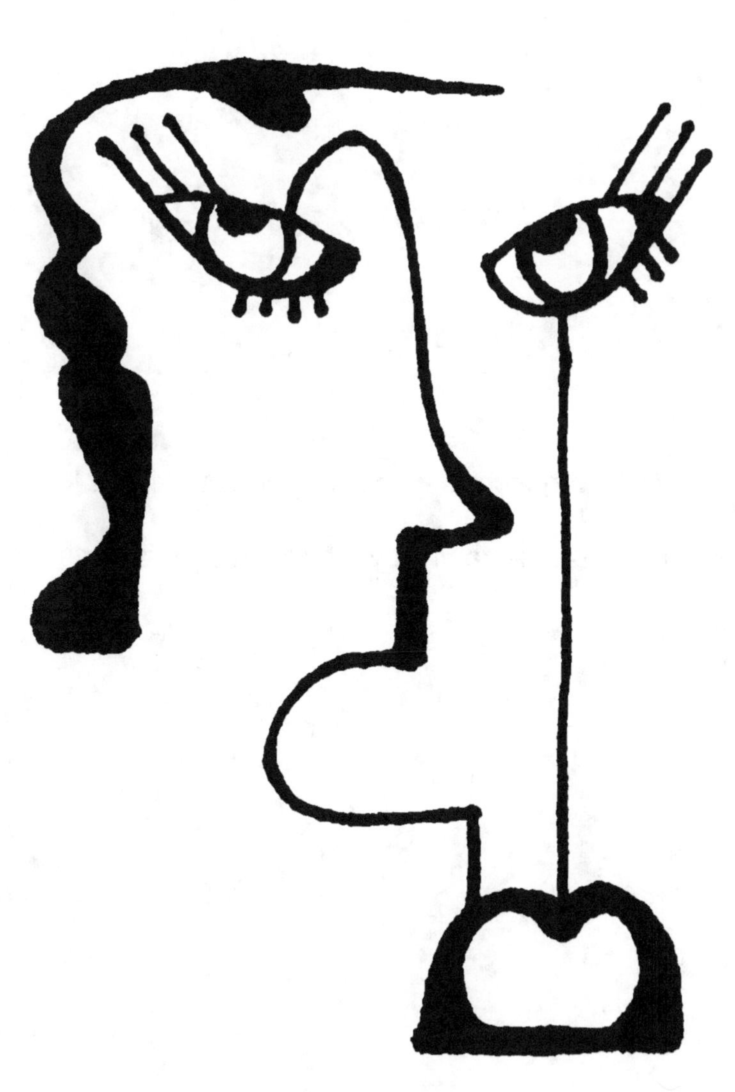

Do you know that chick who is buying you drinks?

No, but she is apparently my afternoon benefactor.

Easy Mike

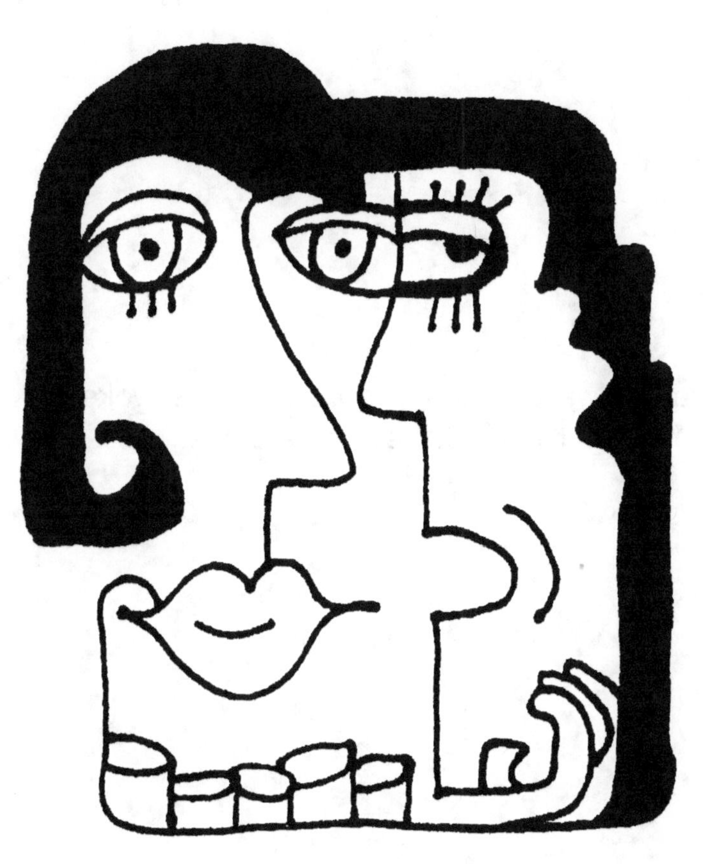

Tuna king walks in and he's like…"Ah, just woke
up and then I thought… let me get a beer."

Erica

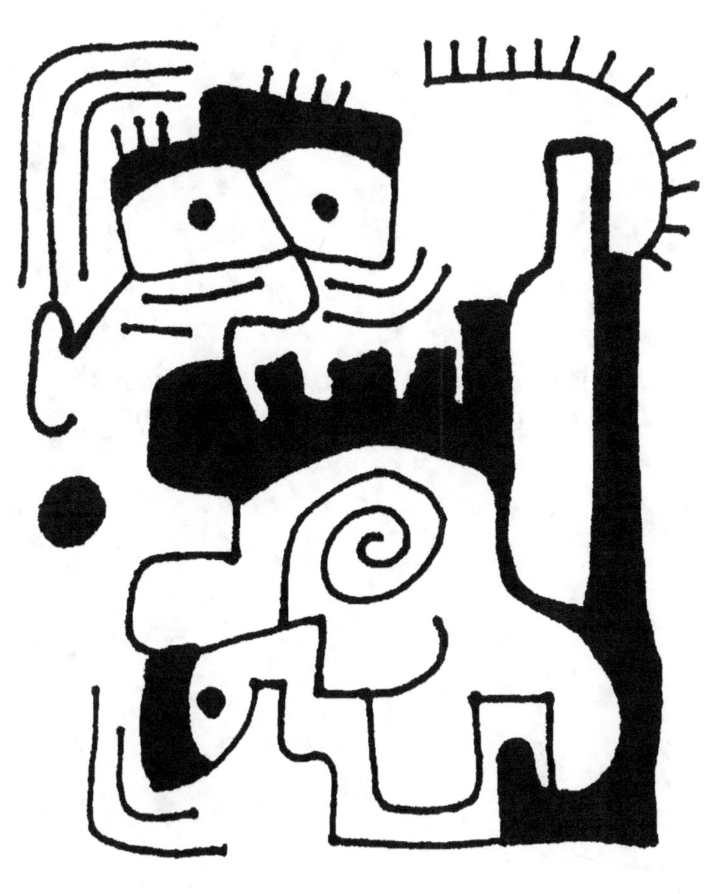

People who likes olives... I mean, why don't they just
suck my ass... your breath would smell the same.

C.F.

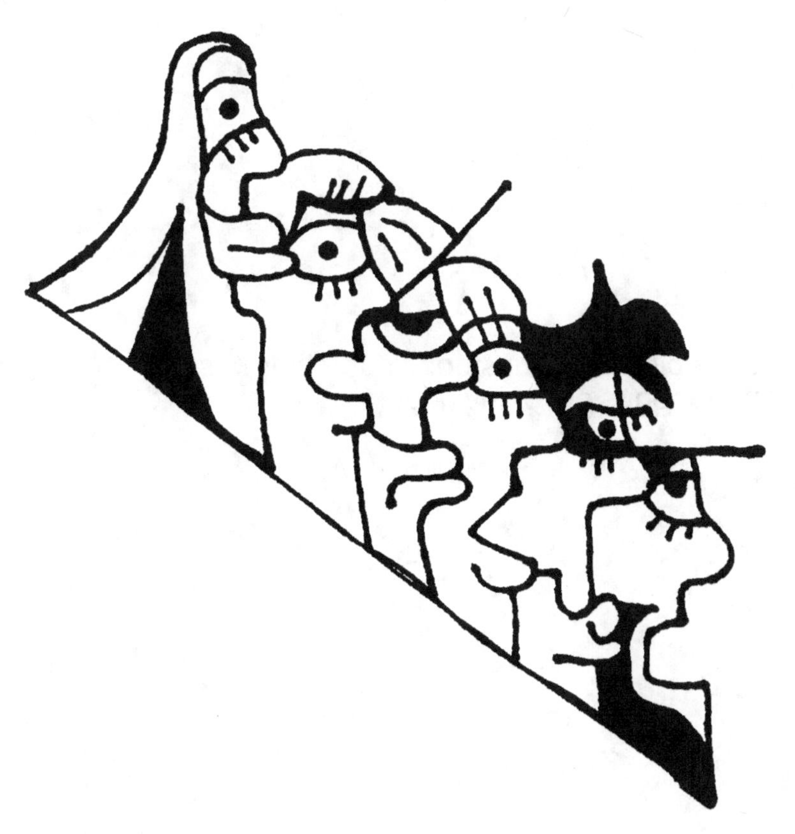

Here's blood in your stool... dude that was
spontaneous out of my head.

Tim

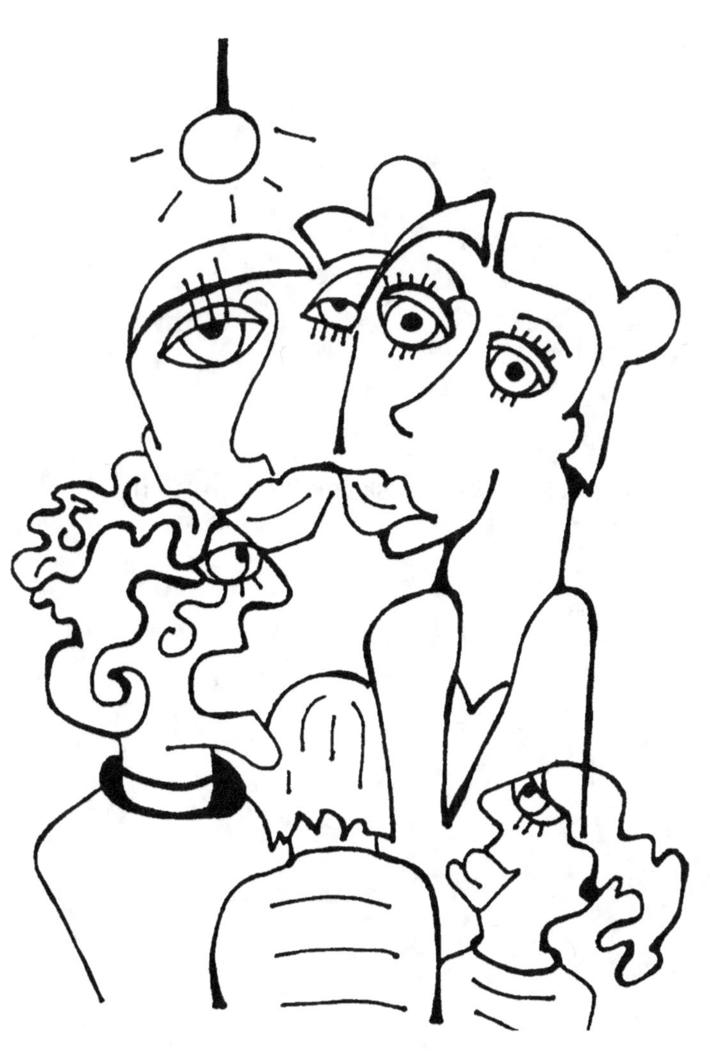

Every time a loser and a skank kiss... an angel wipes his ass.

Christmas Darren

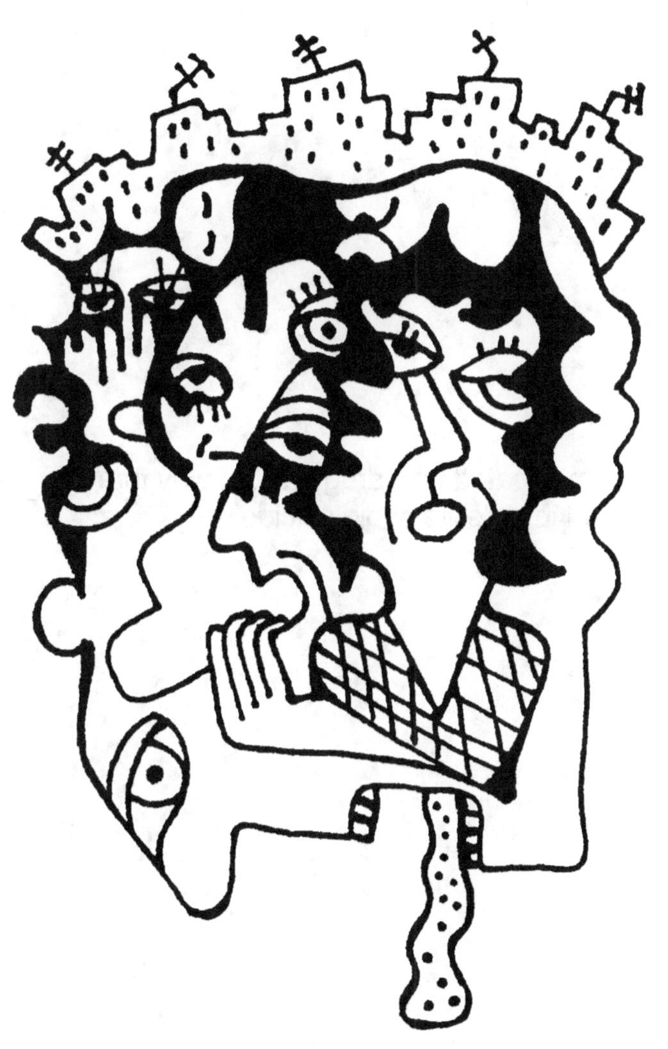

I just self medicated with drugs all the way through high school in order to avoid suicide.

Leslie Mcgiver

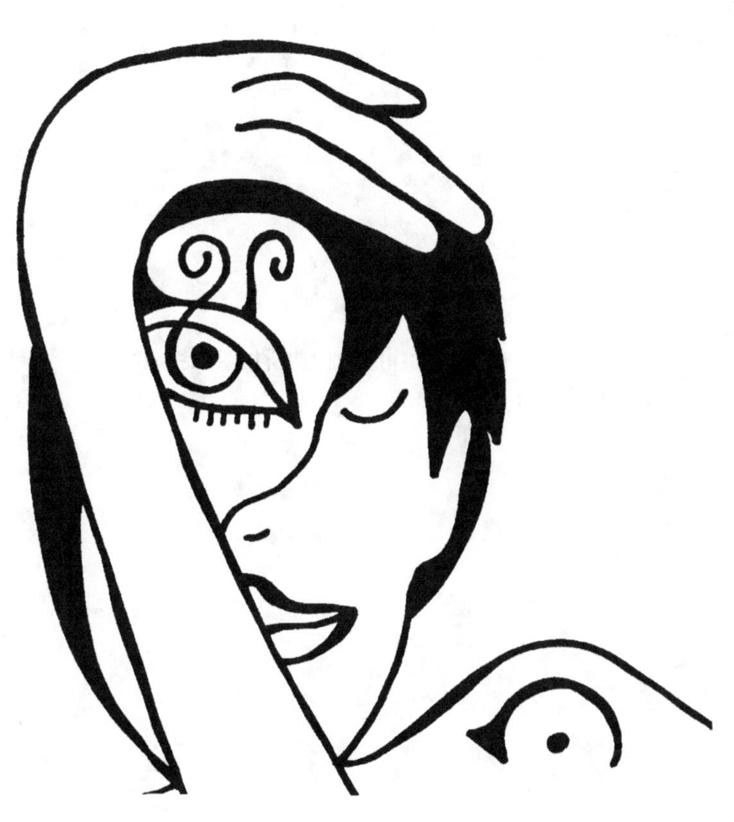

Have you ever seen a chain on a Christmas tree?
...only in the East Village.

Bartender E

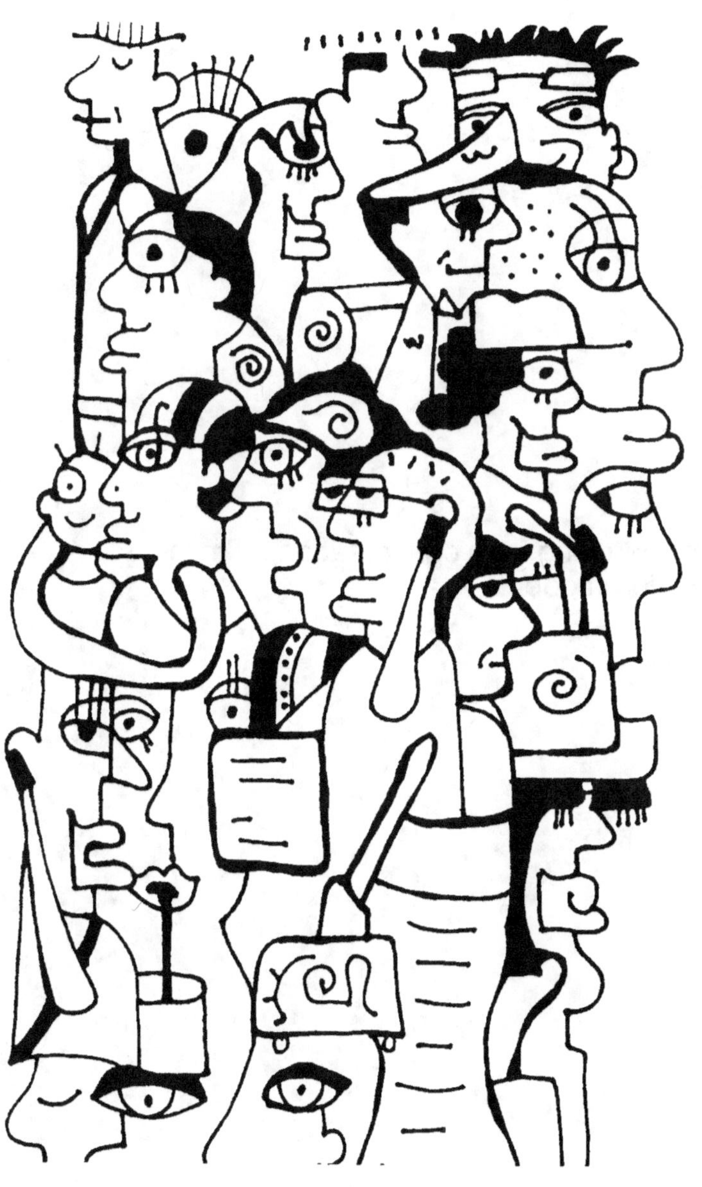

I'm searching for a conversation... I'm in audition mode.

G-fraction

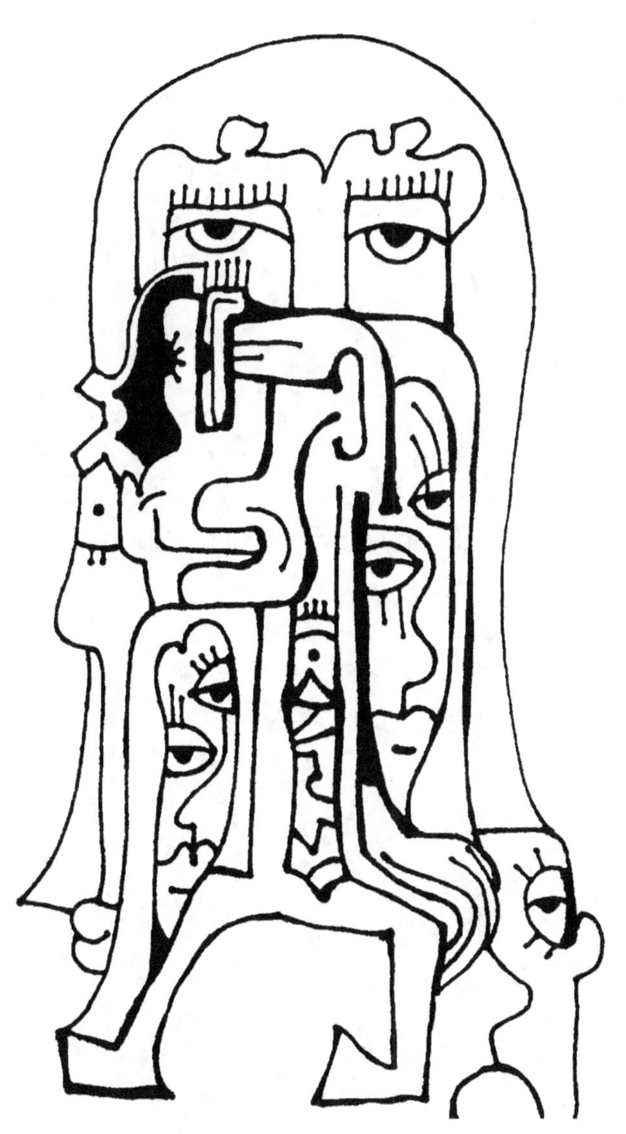

Scotch can beat up any other smell in your mouth.

Rock the Scotchman

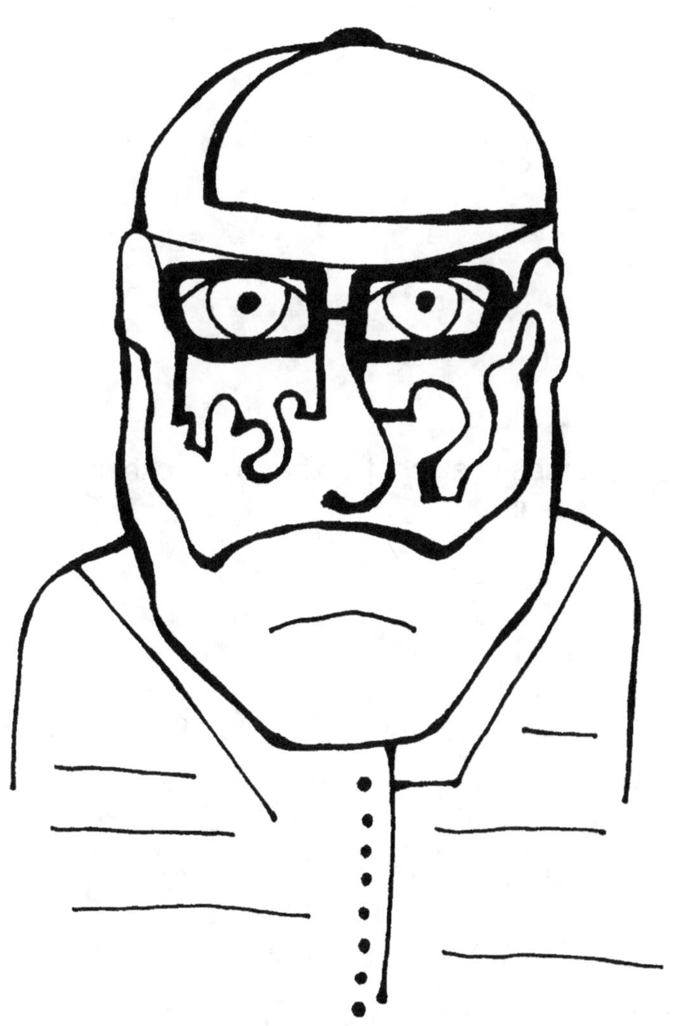

When it comes to alcohol... it has to be either
brown or see through.

JTL

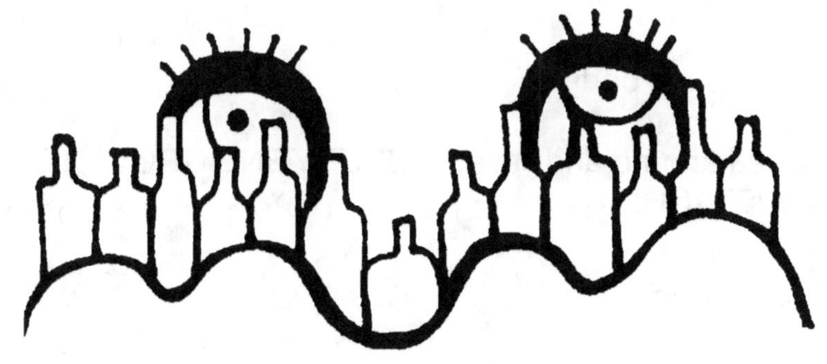

How was the party?

I turned around and yelled... EVERYONE GROW
A MUSTACHE.

Confederate James

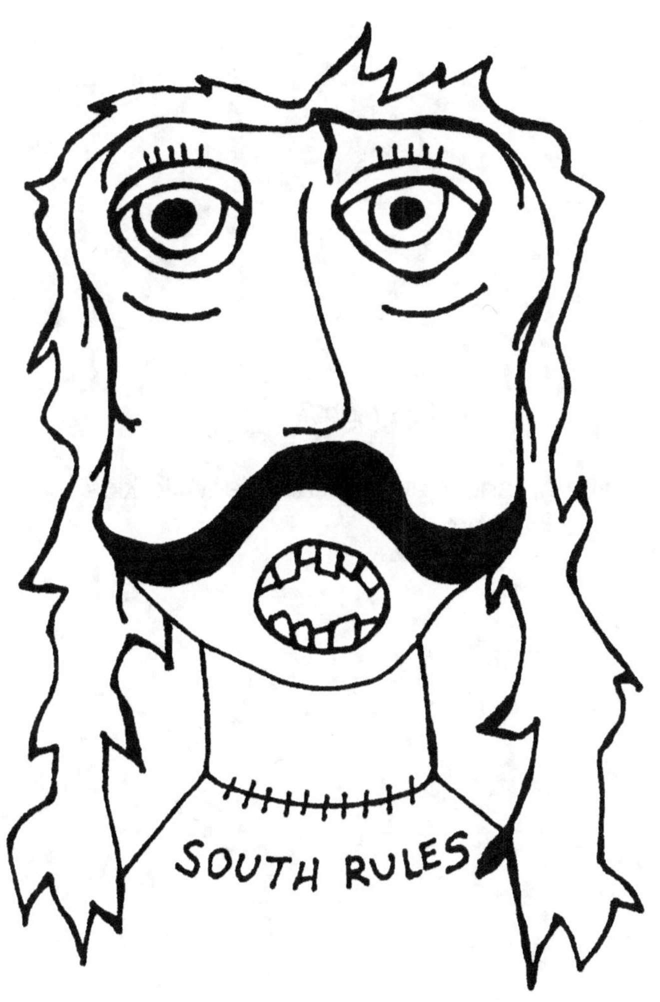
SOUTH RULES

How was the crowd last night?

It was hip hop and they were all little white kids...
I wanted to kill them.

Buddy the Bouncer

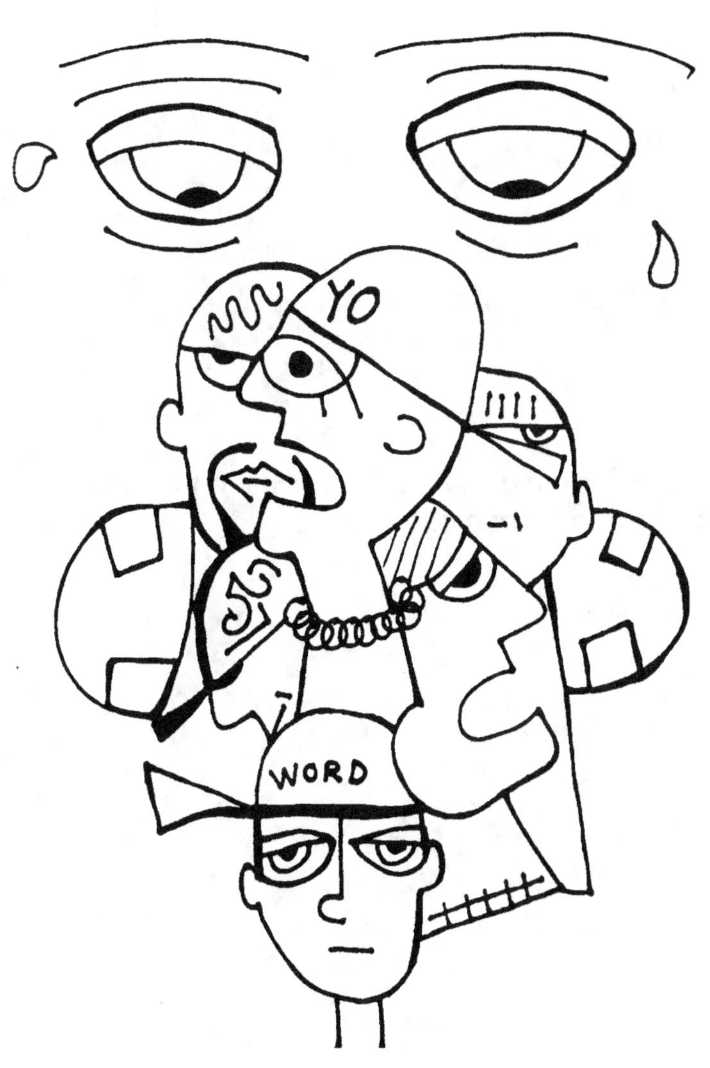

YO
WORD

My father told me never to play poker with a guy
with a city in his name.

Motor City James

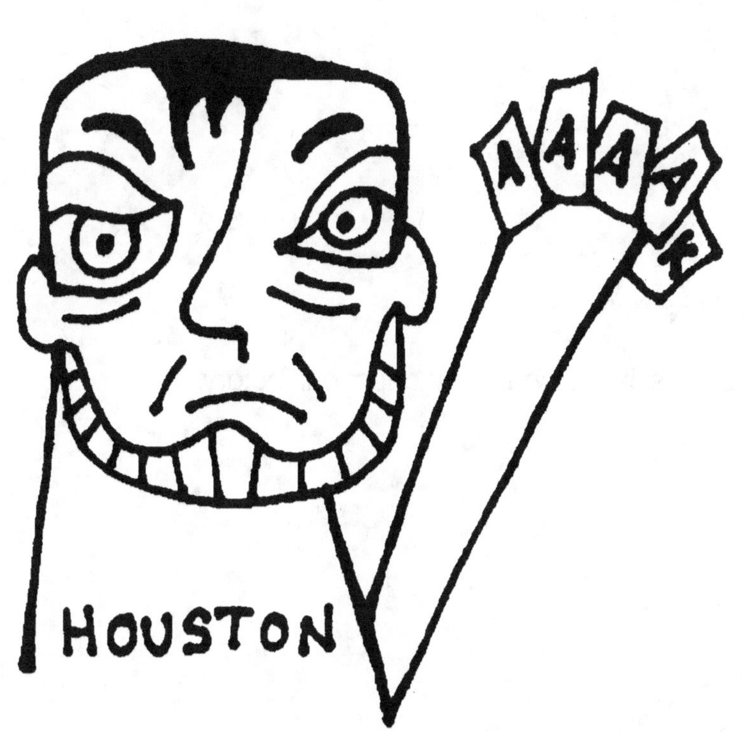

AAAAK
HOUSTON

It stinks here.

It smells like a whale in a chemical factory.

Mike

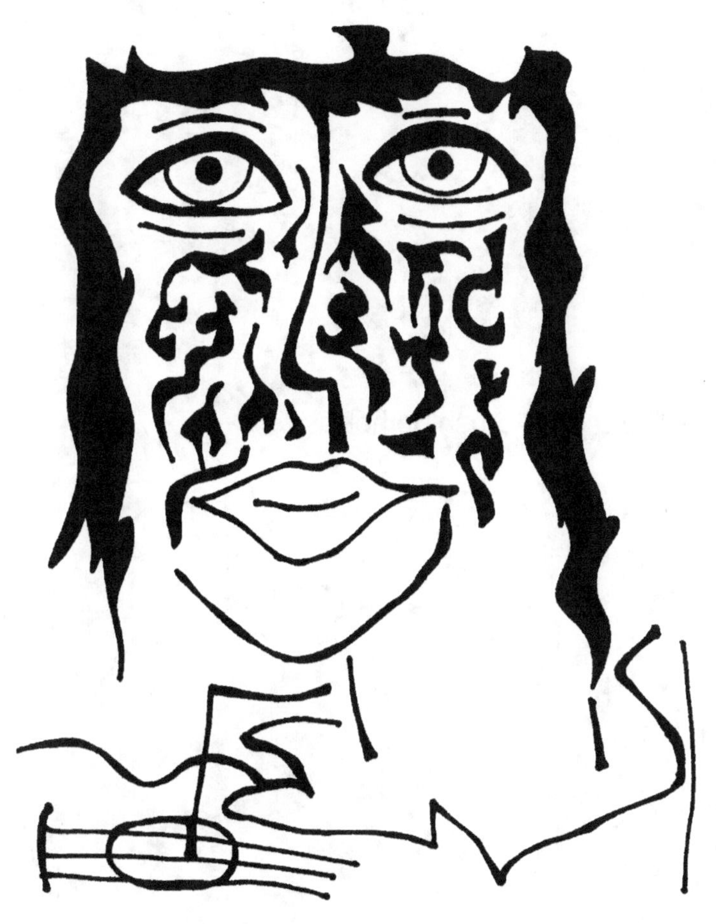

It was like a paint brush up her ass.

Anthony the Artist

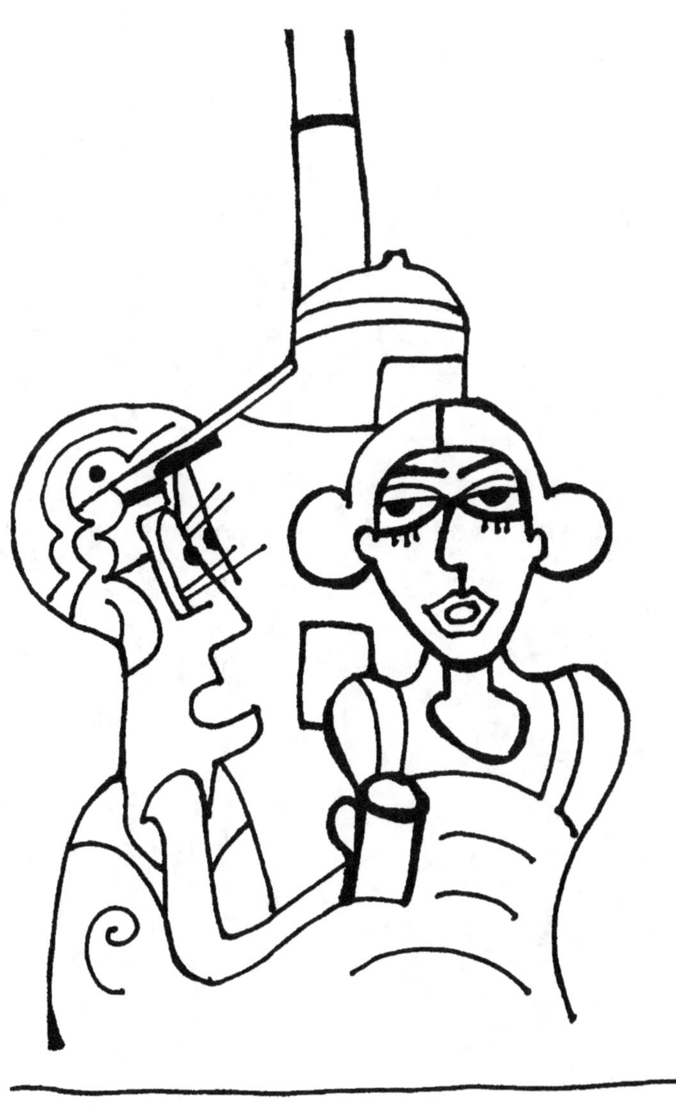

No matter where you're at... happy hour is universal.

DJ Darren

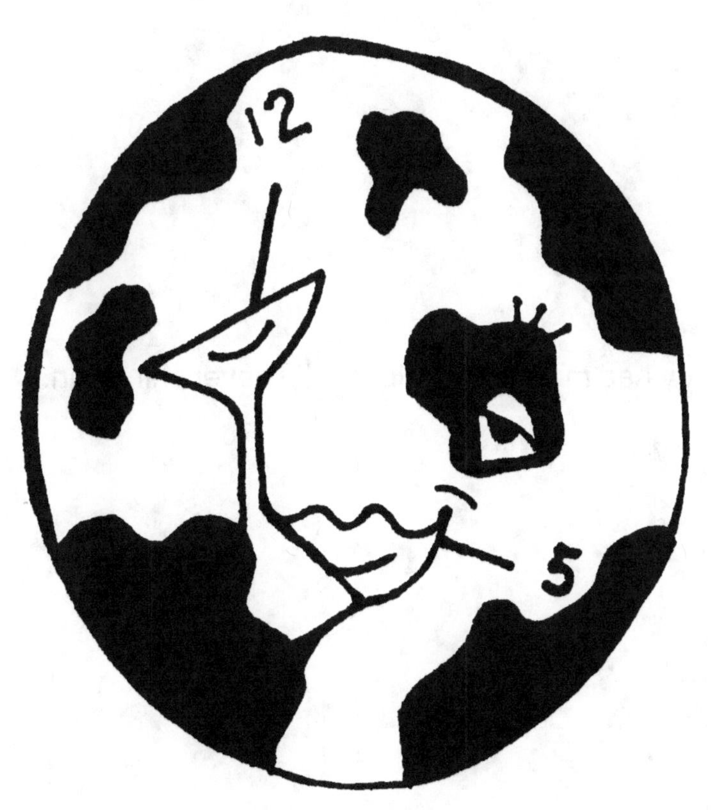

12
5

If they had mozzarella sticks... I'd never shit again.

Greasy Mary

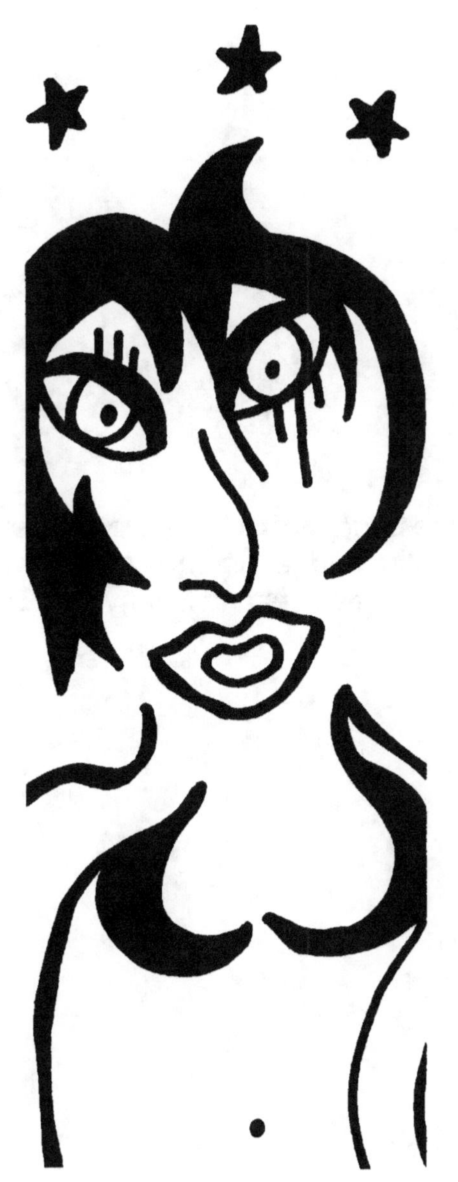

The awesome budget of Scooby-Doo... they
wasted the entire budget on one episode with
the Harlem Globetrotters and Sonny and Cher.

Cartoon Mike

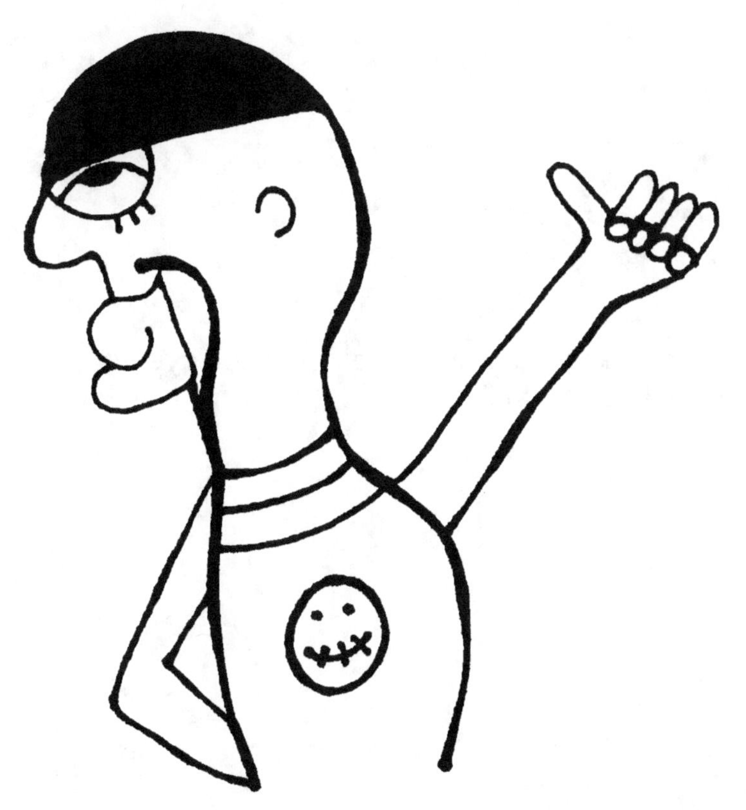

You look betta than Vin Diesel... that took years
of my life to say, fucko.

Anthony the Italian

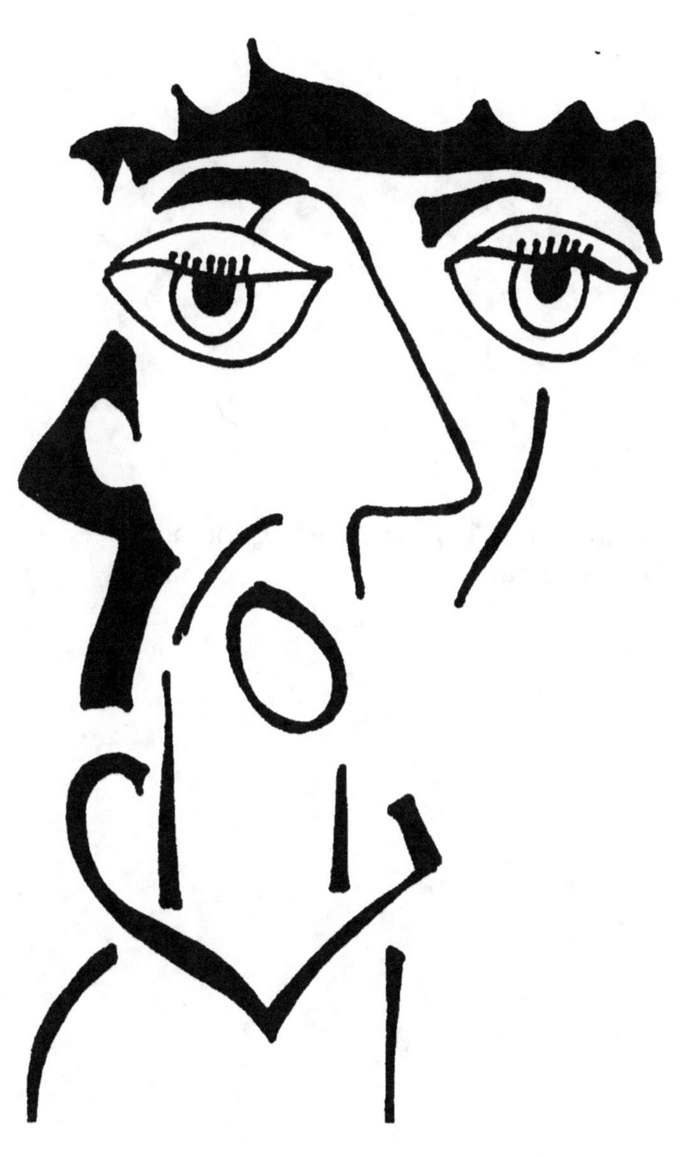

It's not finished... it's a nuclear exploding martini glass tattoo.

Rock

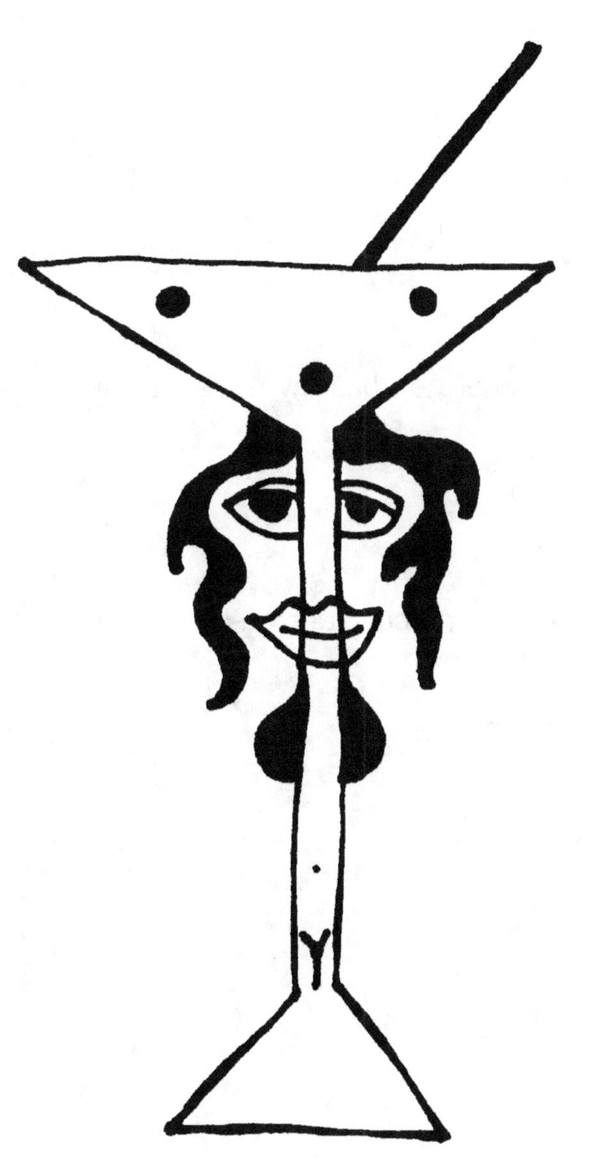

Mary, you smell good... maybe it's the shellac.

How do you smell spellack?

G-Man

You've had too much to drink... did you mean spell shellac?

Too much pressure.

G-Man

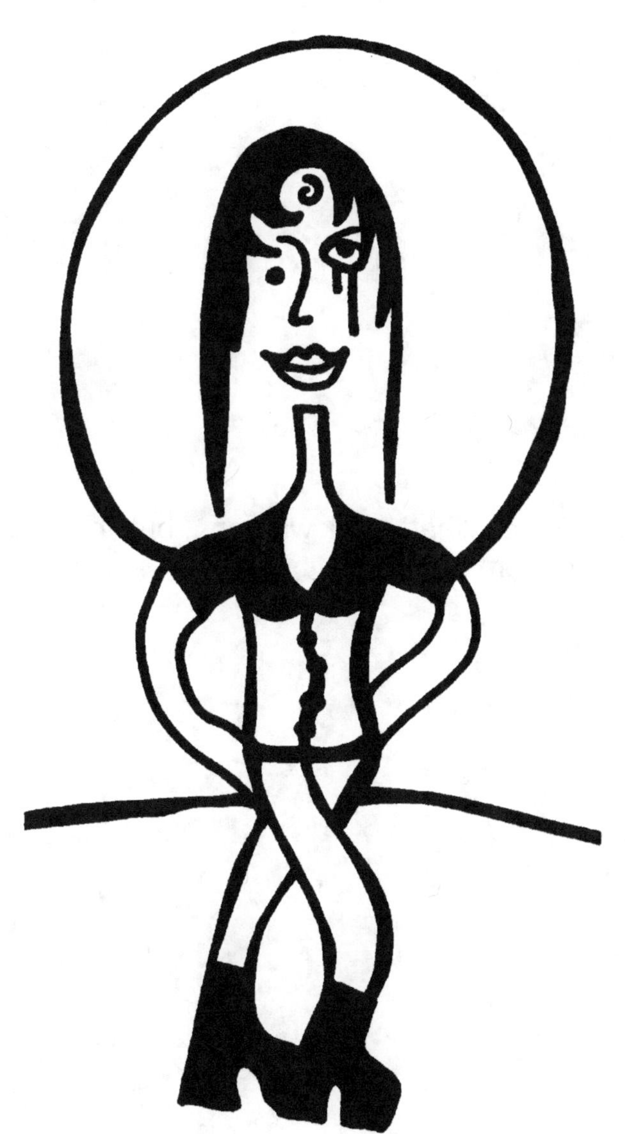

You may have all had black women... but you
never had them on the continent.

African James

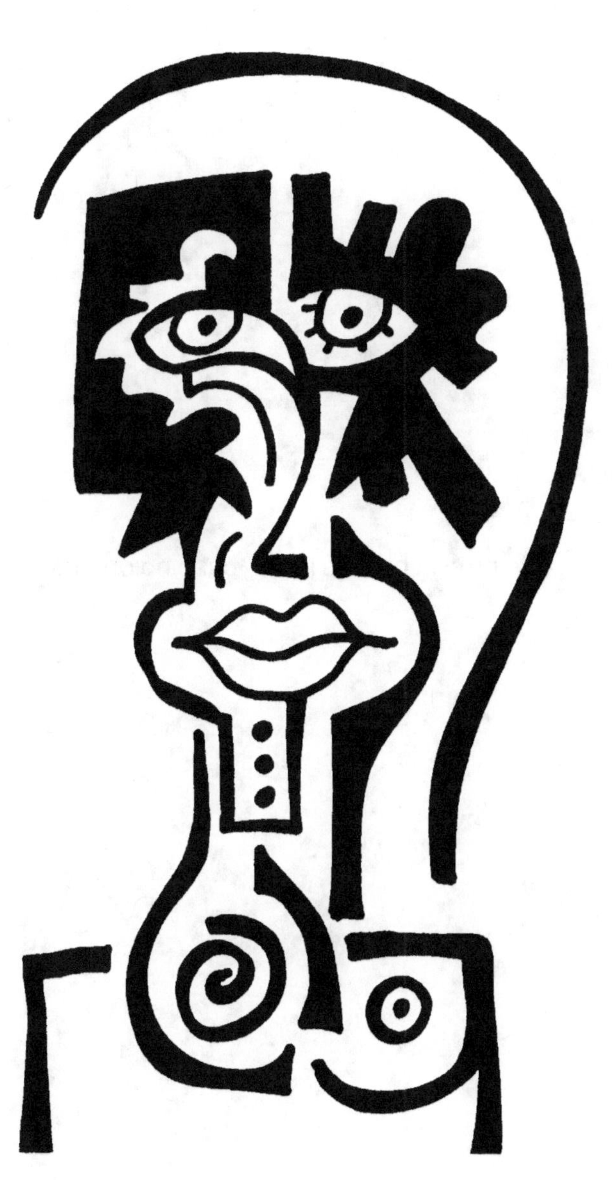

He had a cattle prod in his cab just in case no one paid.

James

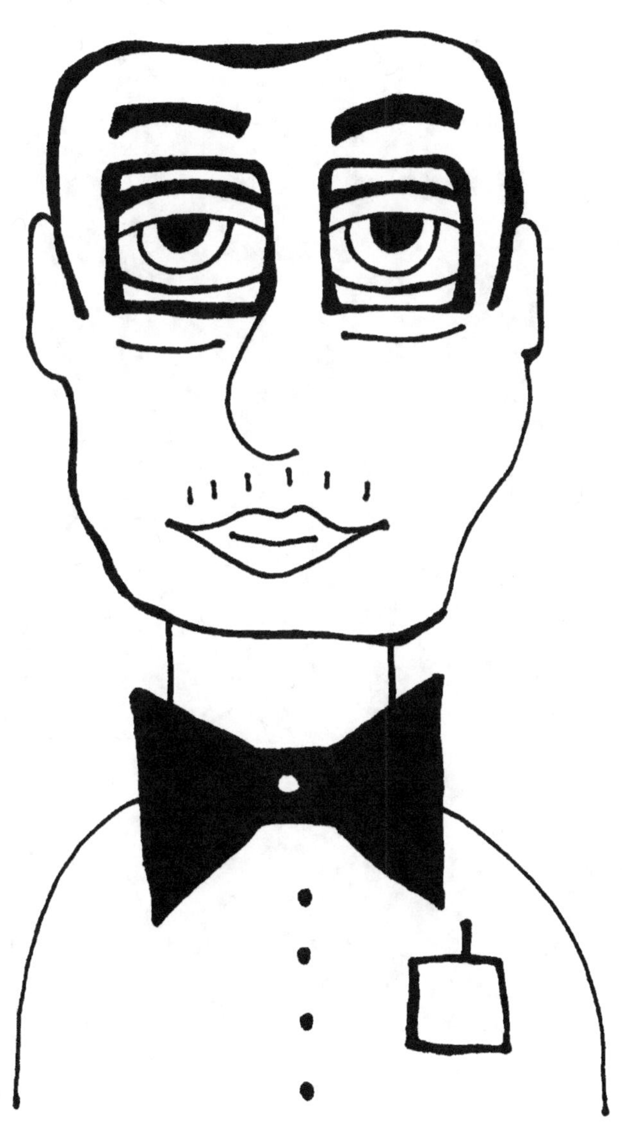

everyday life

You're ready to attack the day and then you see a
guy taking a shit between two cars... that slows
you down.

Bobby Pinn

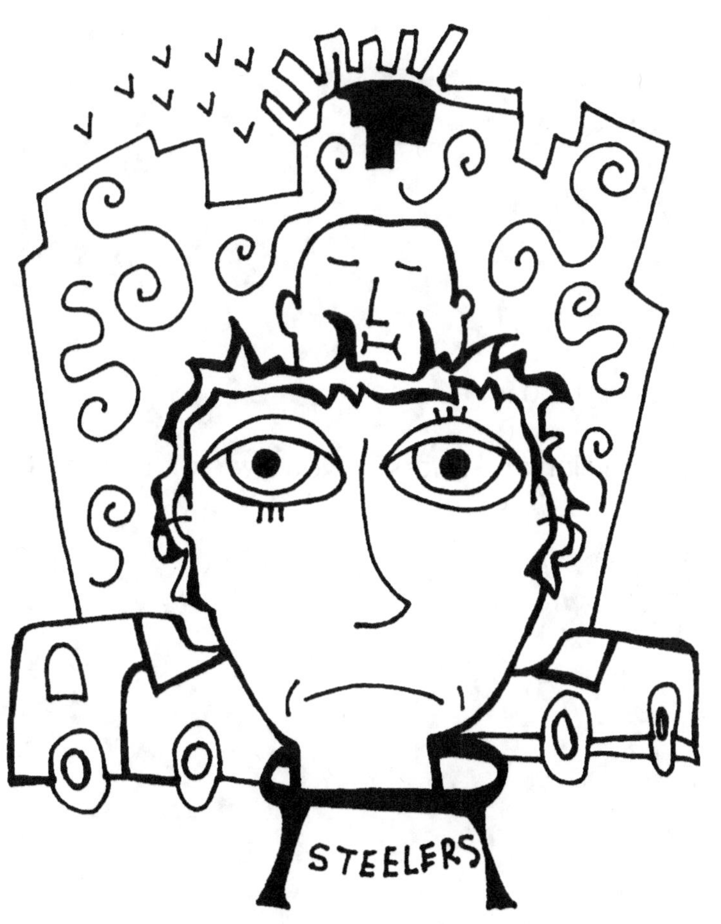

STEELERS

What do you do for a living?

I'm a magician and I work at Newsweek... So fuck it.

Magician Steve

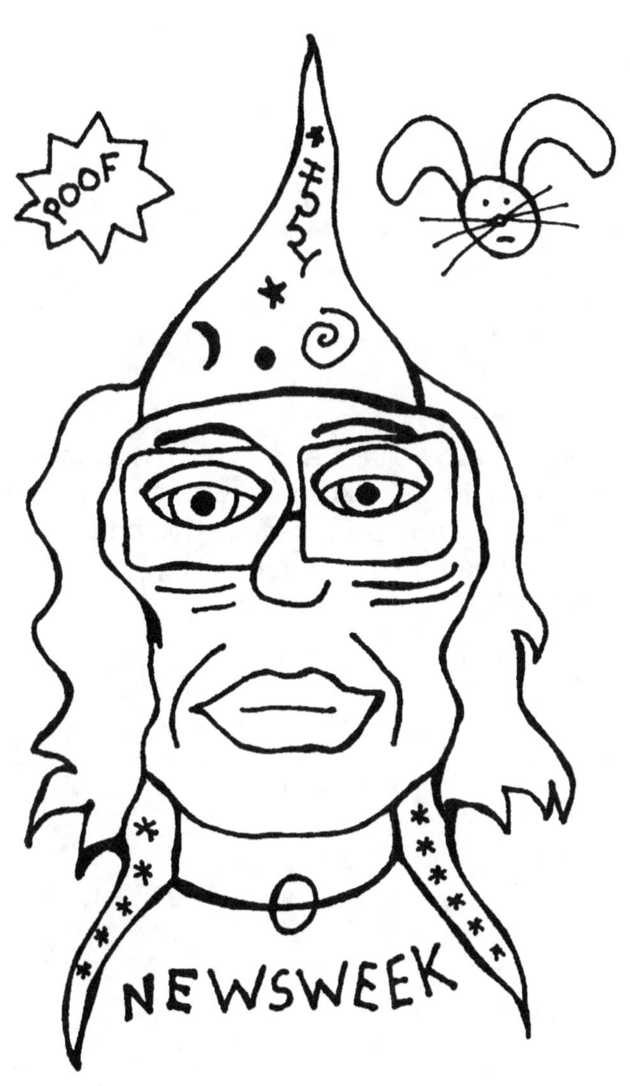

POOF
NEWSWEEK

He did something revolutionary in sound design, so
I asked him what his background was and he said
he won a fourth grade science fair... his project
was a five volt battery and a number two pencil
and it illuminated the room.

Ron

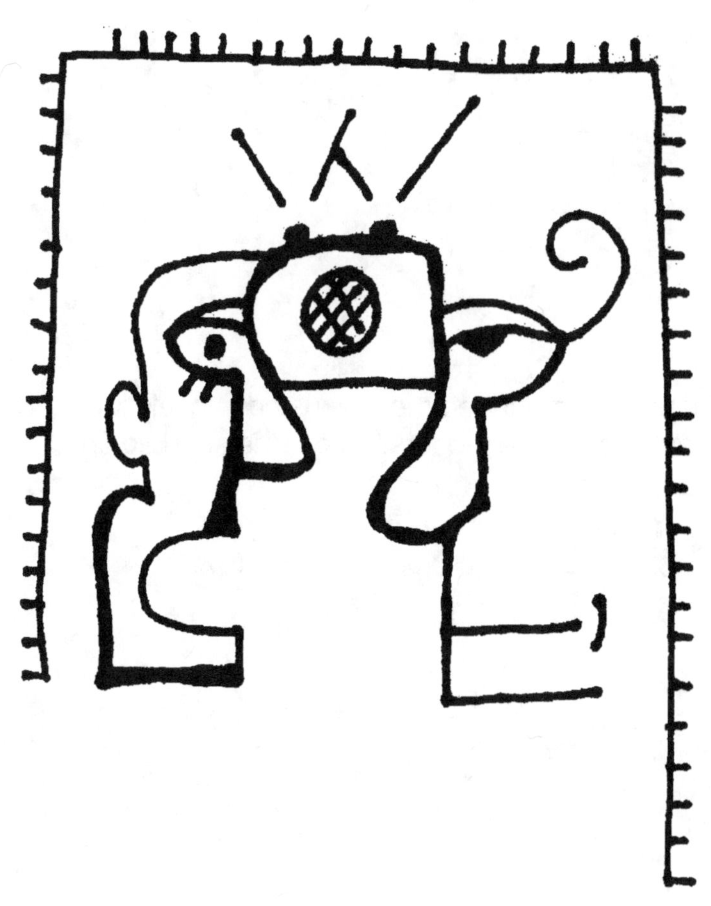

When my dad handed me the rusted shovel I knew
it was time to hide the torso under the shed again.

Mysterious Mike

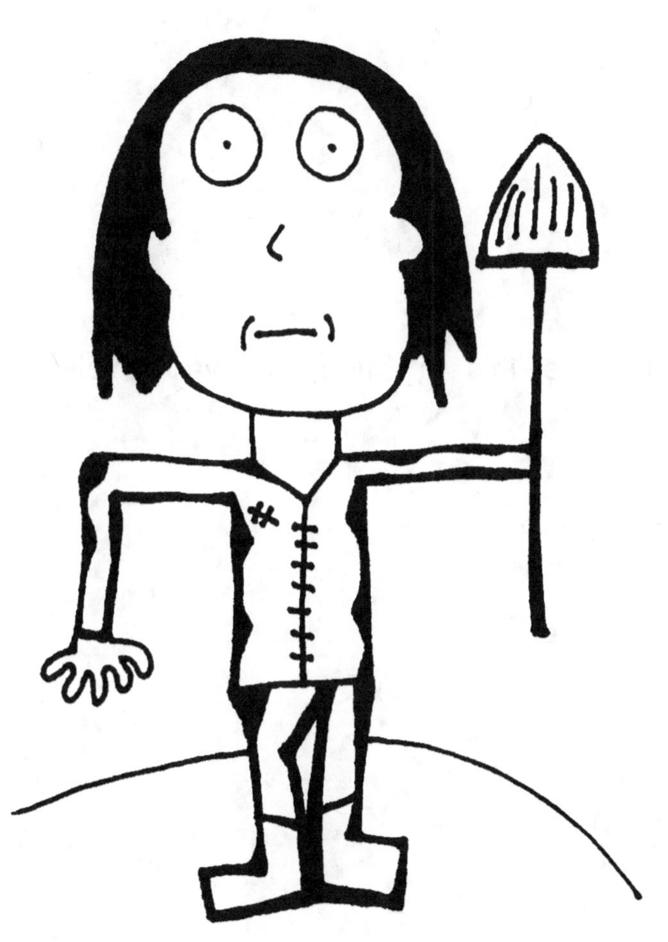

You don't see this very often... a vulva in a Volvo.

M.R.

What's a vulva?

Maartje

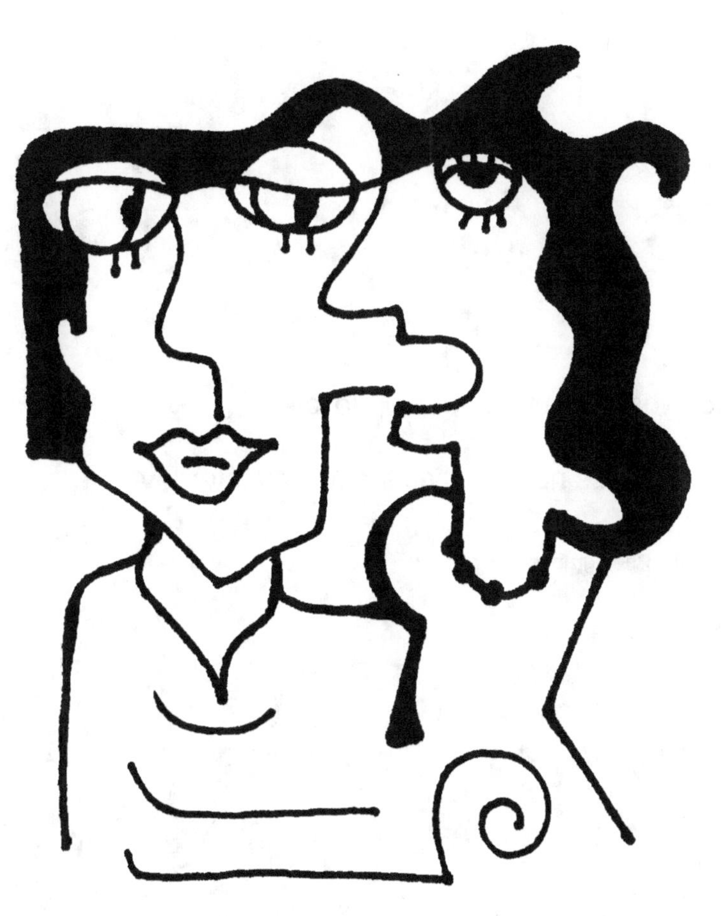

So, what have you been up to lately?

I took a piss next to my cube truck yesterday.

Frag the Photographer

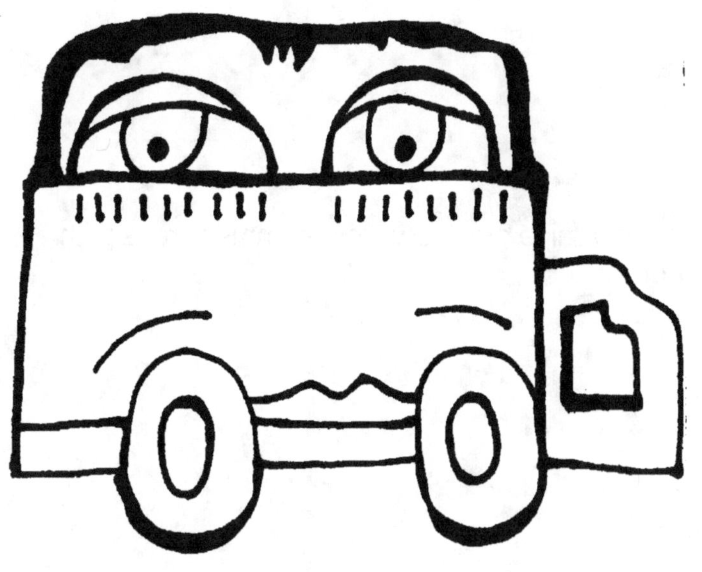

You want a nice girl in a yellow summer dress with
big hooters.

John the Lawyer

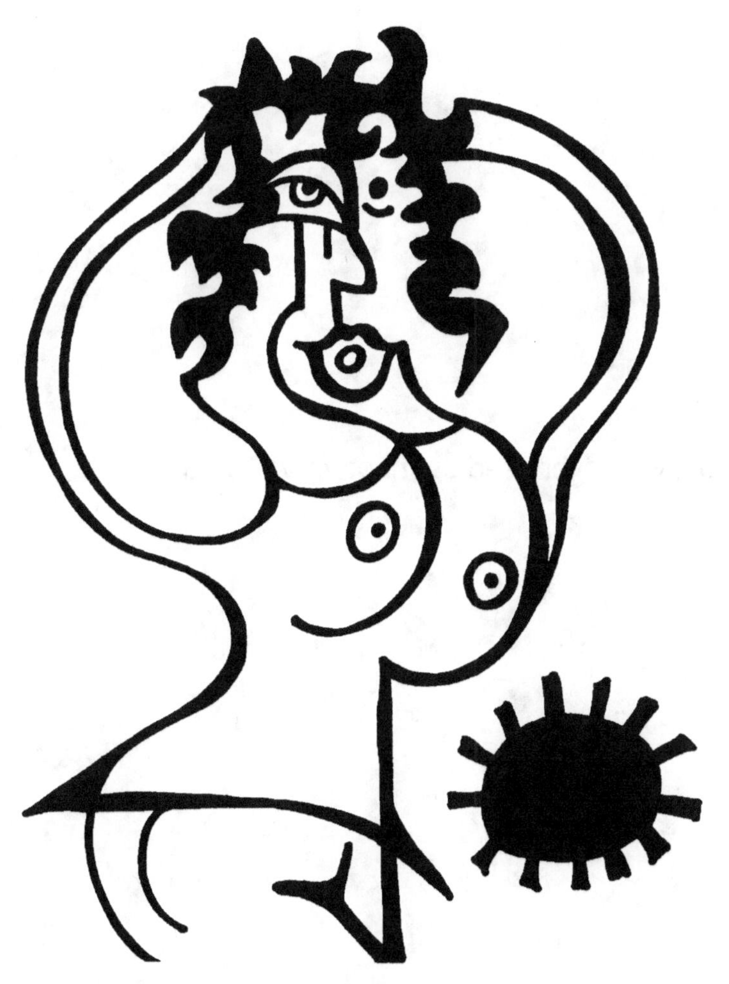

Dude, we never used our hooters VIP cards.

Stoner

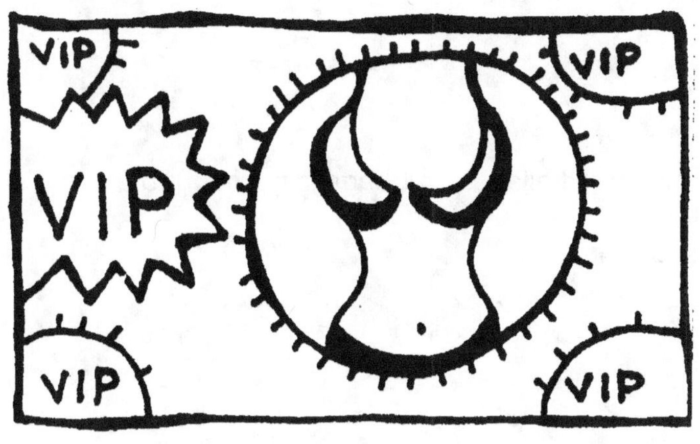

VIP
VIP
VIP
VIP
VIP

Honey, we're Italians... cabbage is not in our diet.

Mary Fragapane

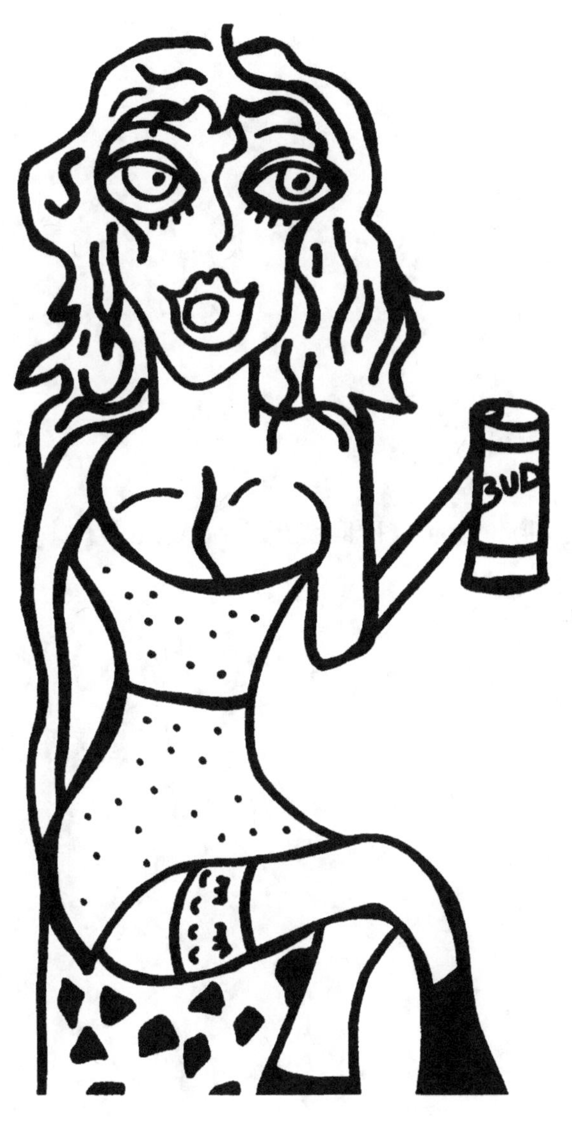
BUD

Drinking black coffee is like drinking feet.

Nephew Mike

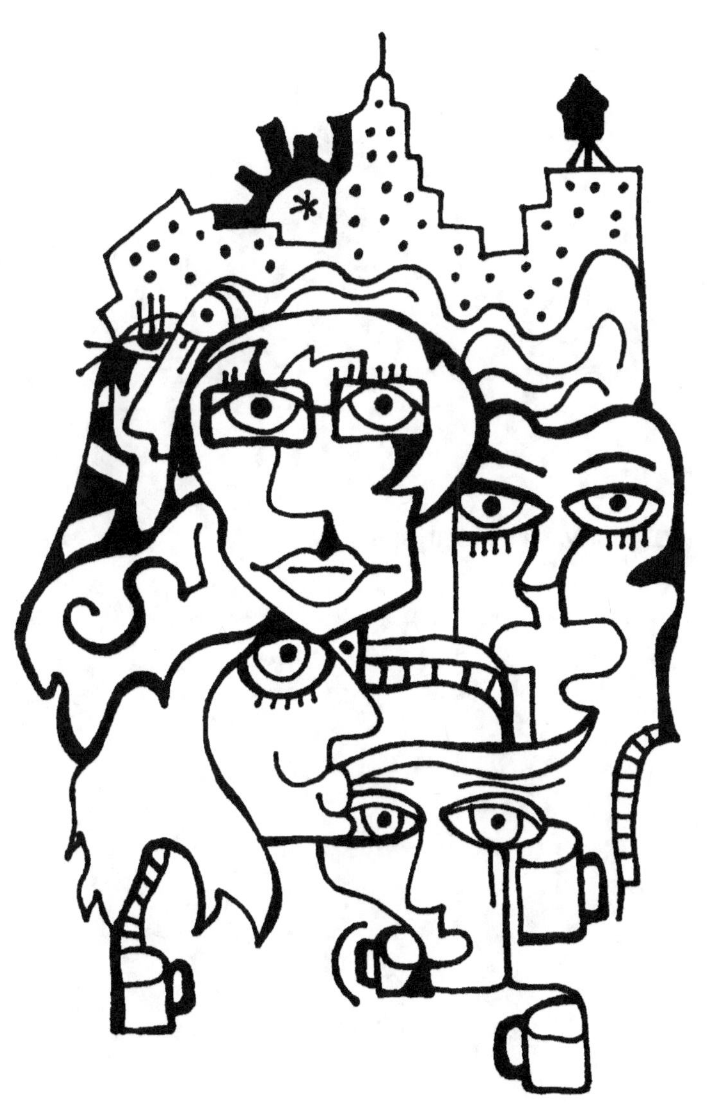

I'm not lucky... I'm fearless.

Kevin the Producer

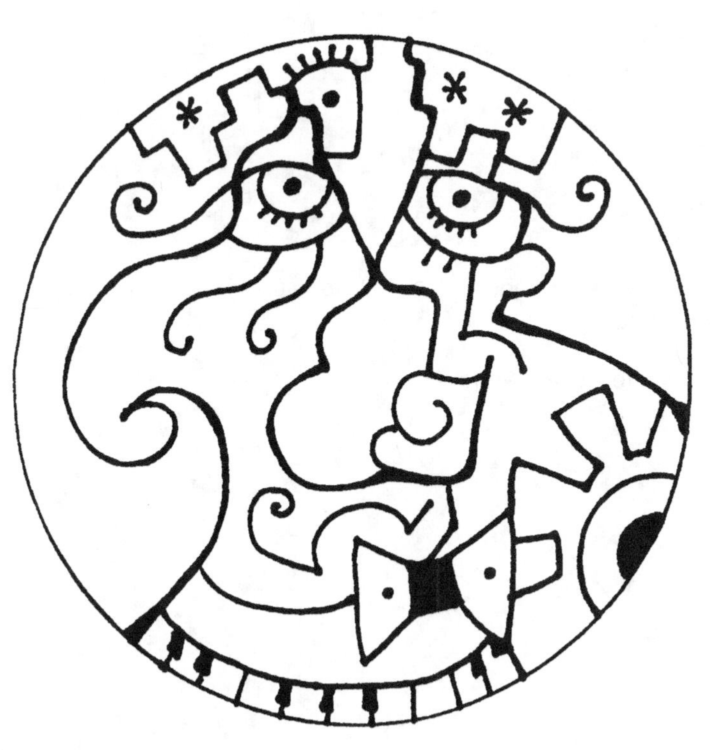

I go to bed with earrings and when I wake up...
they're gone.

Do you have a spare earring?

Canarsie Ken

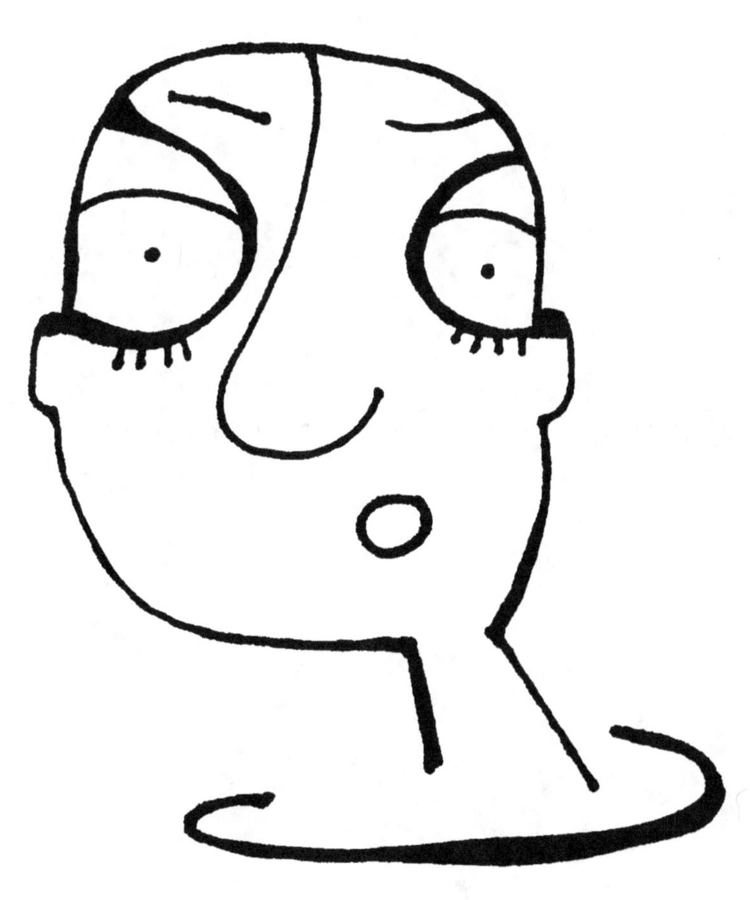

You know I'm flush when I have cheese in the house.

Primary Girl

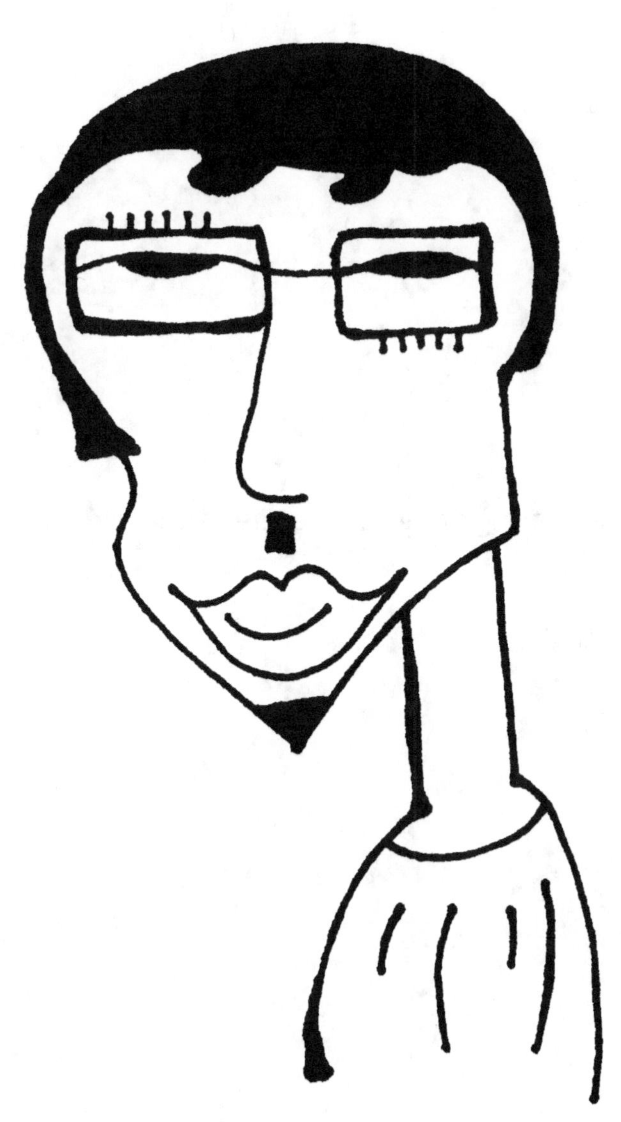

I've been having great transvestite karma all week long.

Makeover Mary

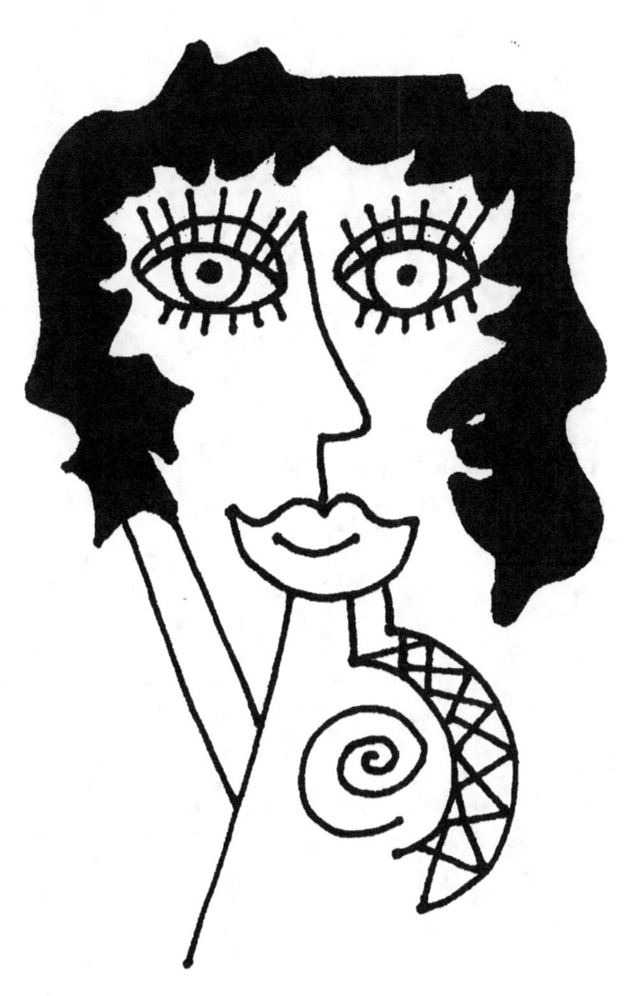

A good friend will help you move... a great friend will help you move a body.

Christopher

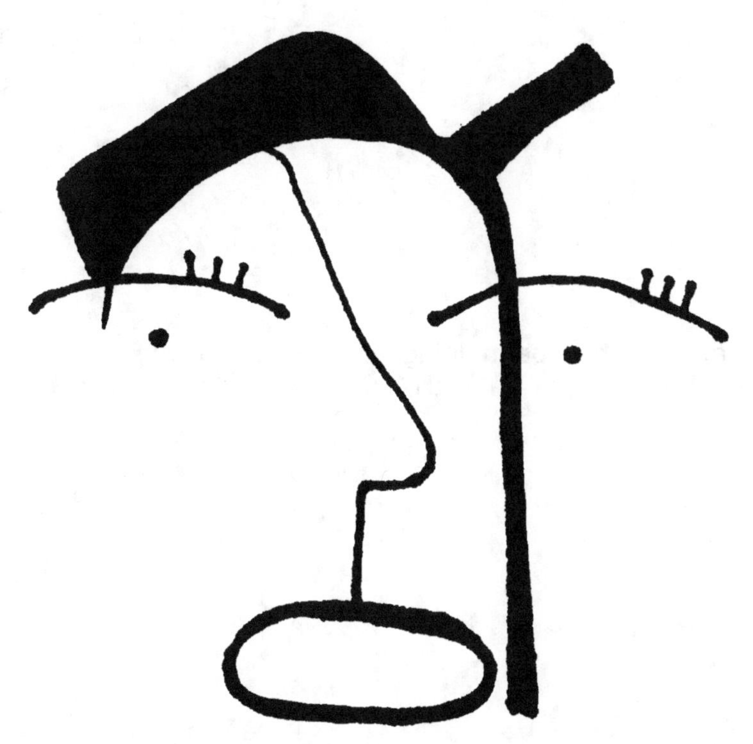

Letterman... he's been doing this since the days I came home trippin' on acid on a school night.

M.F.

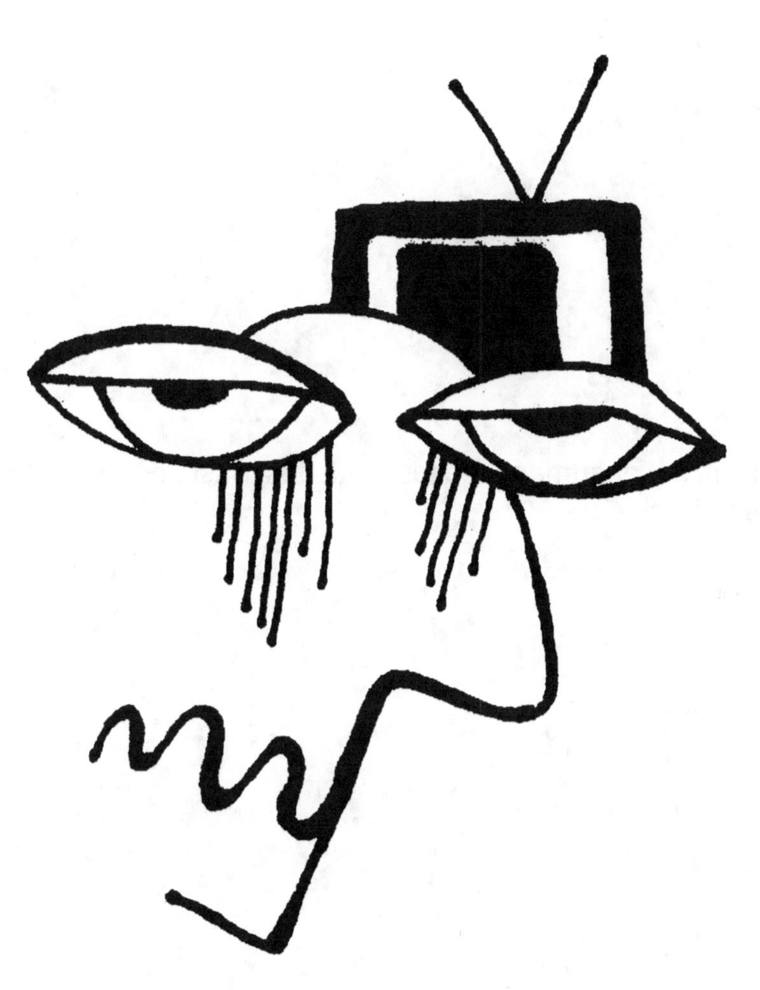

I lost my apartment because I ate his roast beef sandwich.

Anonymous

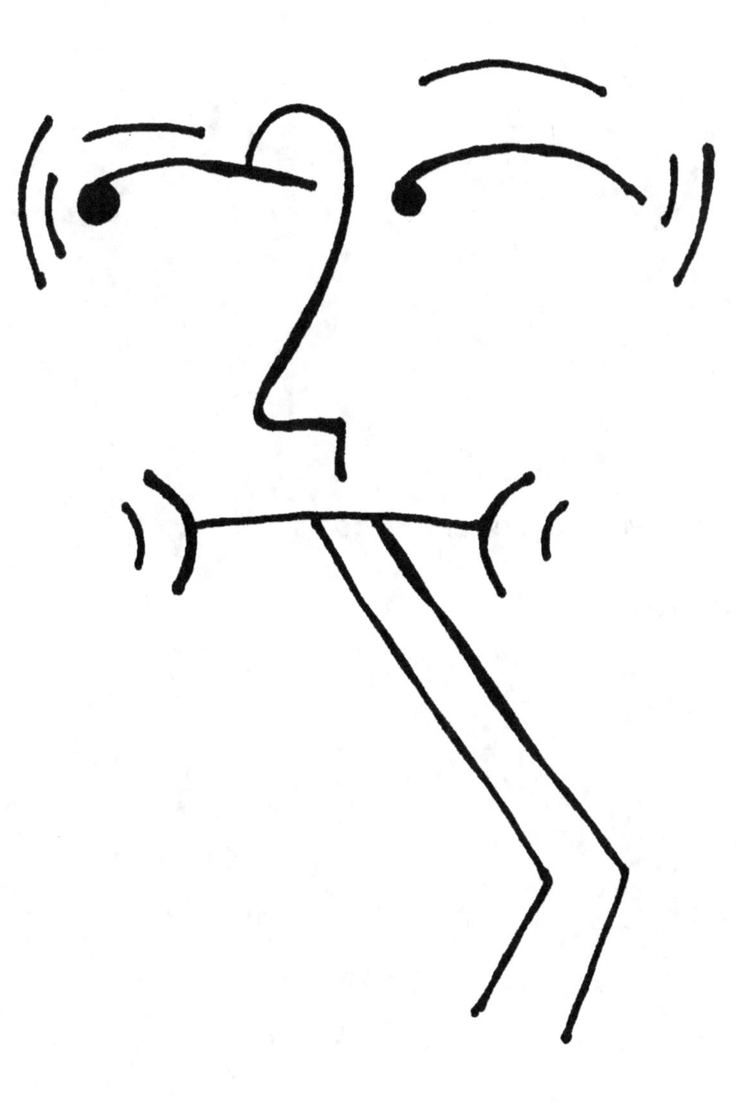

I'm not worried... no career goals.

Bald Cable Guy

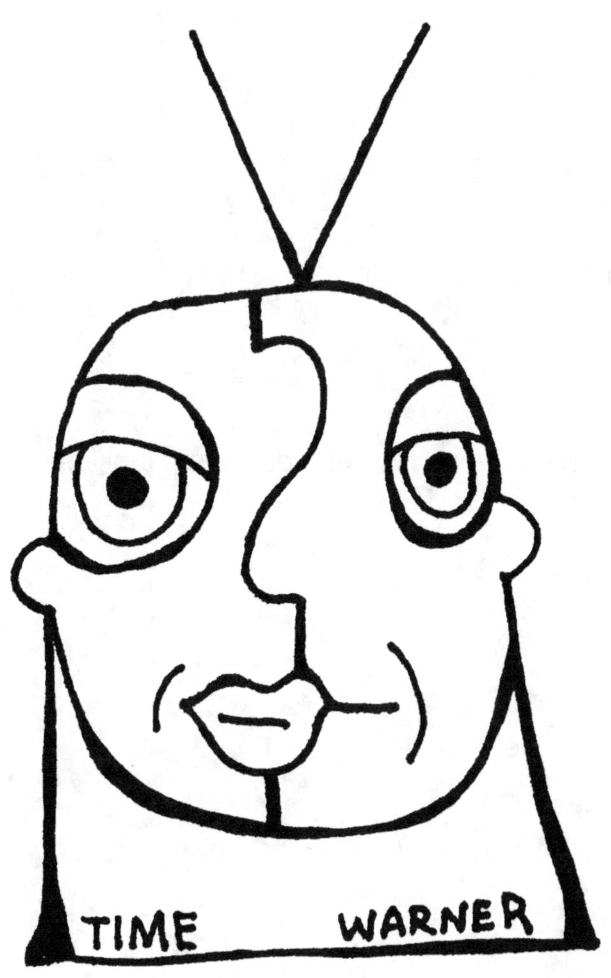

TIME
WARNER

I liked it better when my neighbors were junkies and whores.

East Village Mike

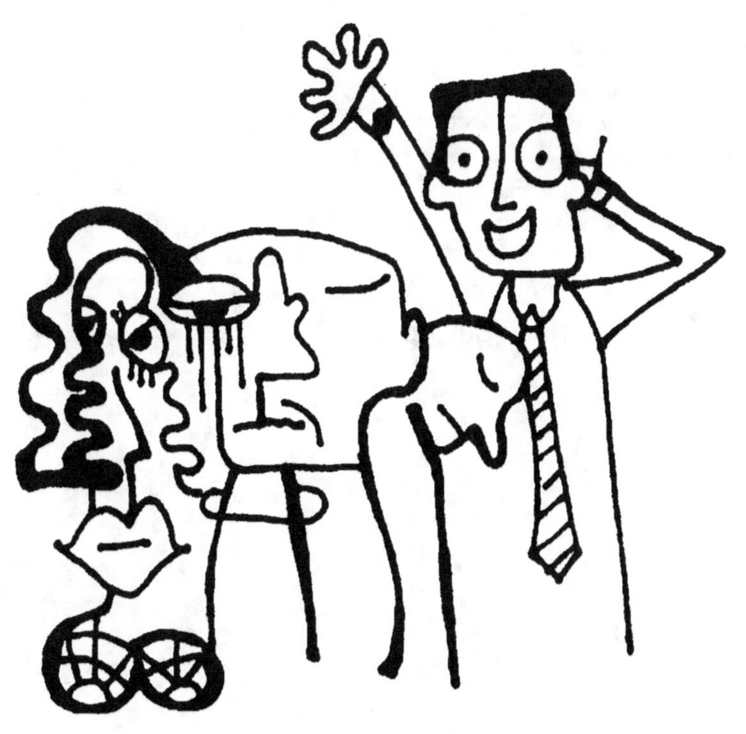

My Chinese crutch guy got off.

John the Lawyer

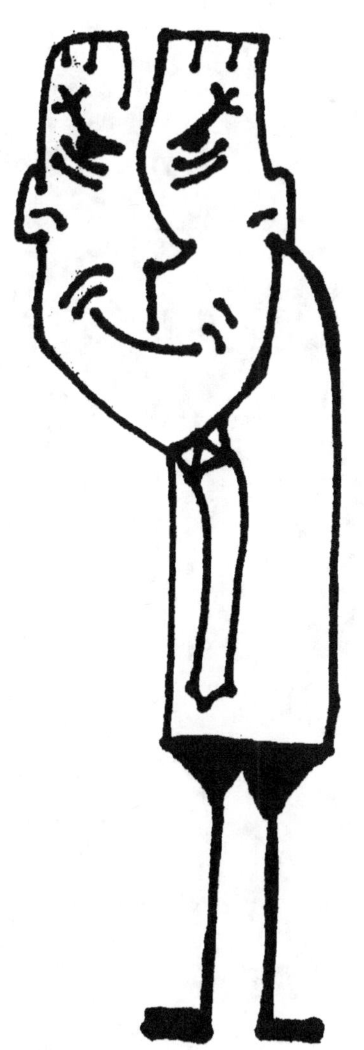

dating

Why don't you go out with him?

I can't date a guy whose ass is smaller than mine.

Uptown Meg

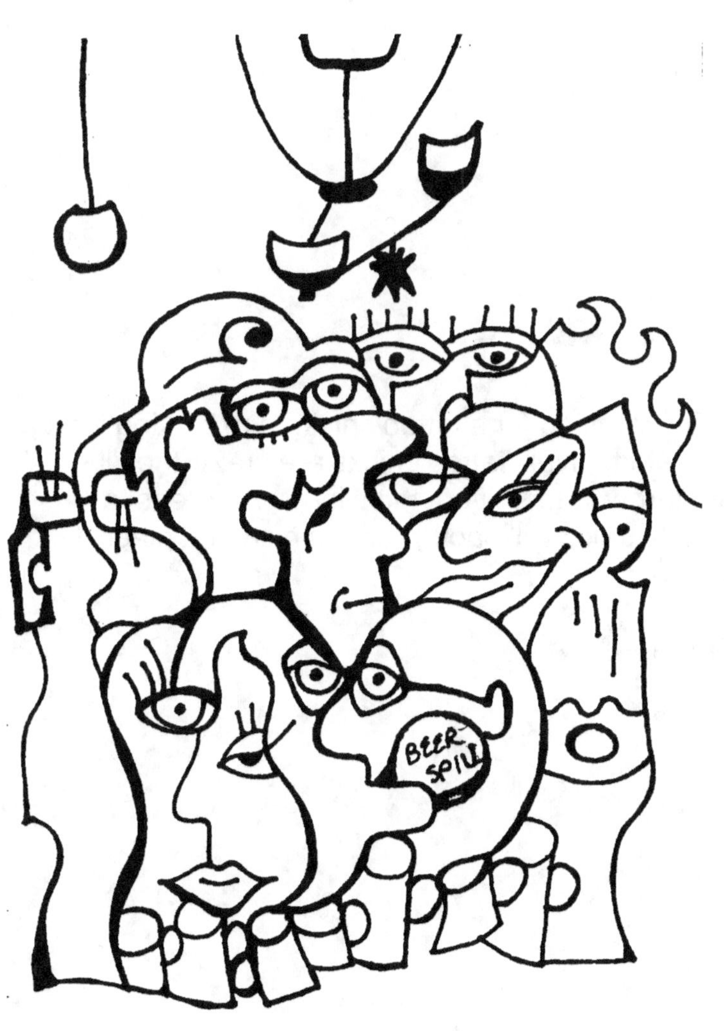

BEER
SPILL

I'm not looking for a tattoo chick… I'm looking for an eight to fiver. Tattoo chicks are crazy, they'll just throw your shit out the window… at least a cubicle chick will pack your shit nice and place it outside.

Line the Tattoo Artist

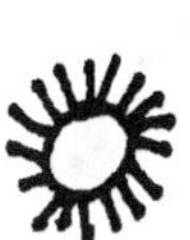
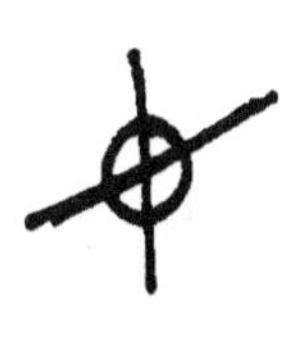
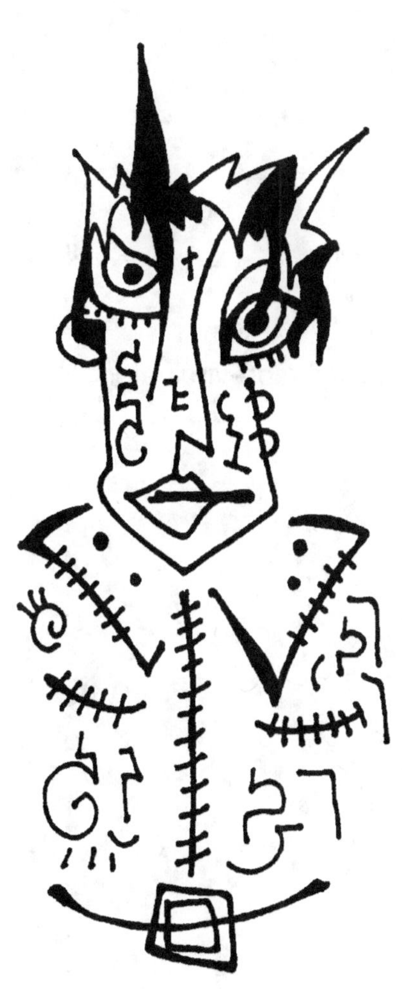

My ex-boyfriend was a de-virginator.

Anonymous chick

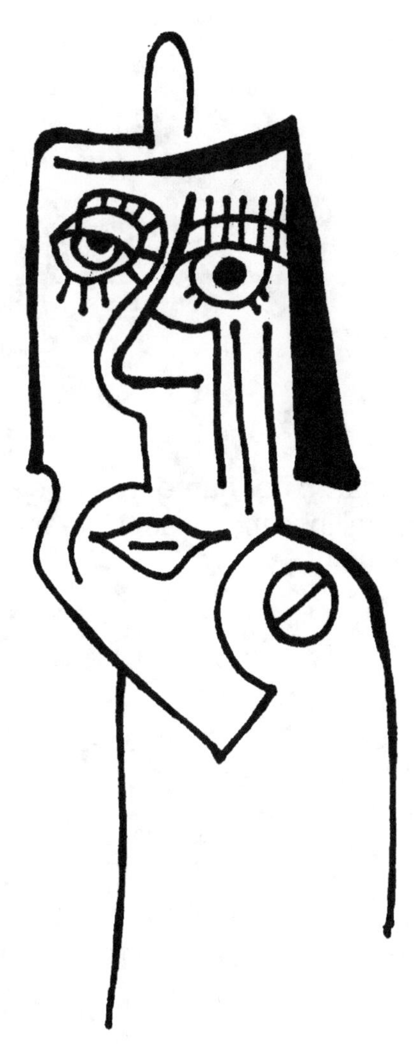

Yipsilanti, Michigan... her name was Speed
Queen... I was ballin' her... I was 23 years old...
man, it was beautiful.

Peter at 50

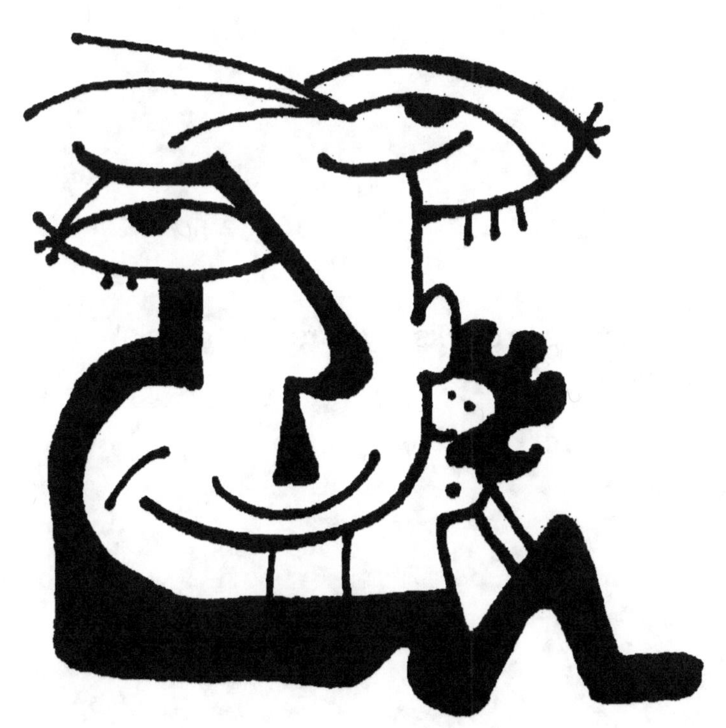

When it comes to chicks... you're either fishin'
or catchin'.

Freez

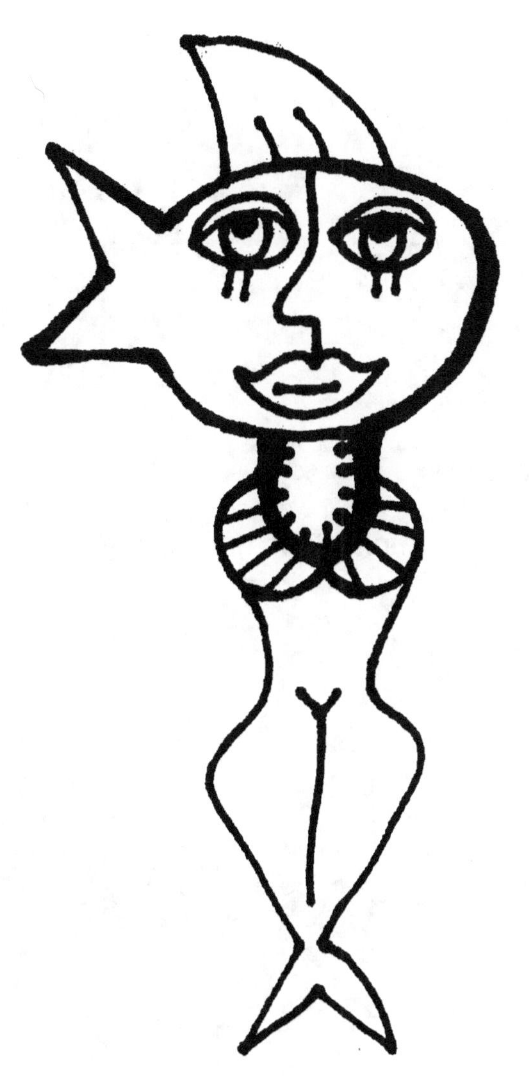

What was she like?

She had hairy armpits... I'm not into that
Sasquatch thing.

M.R.

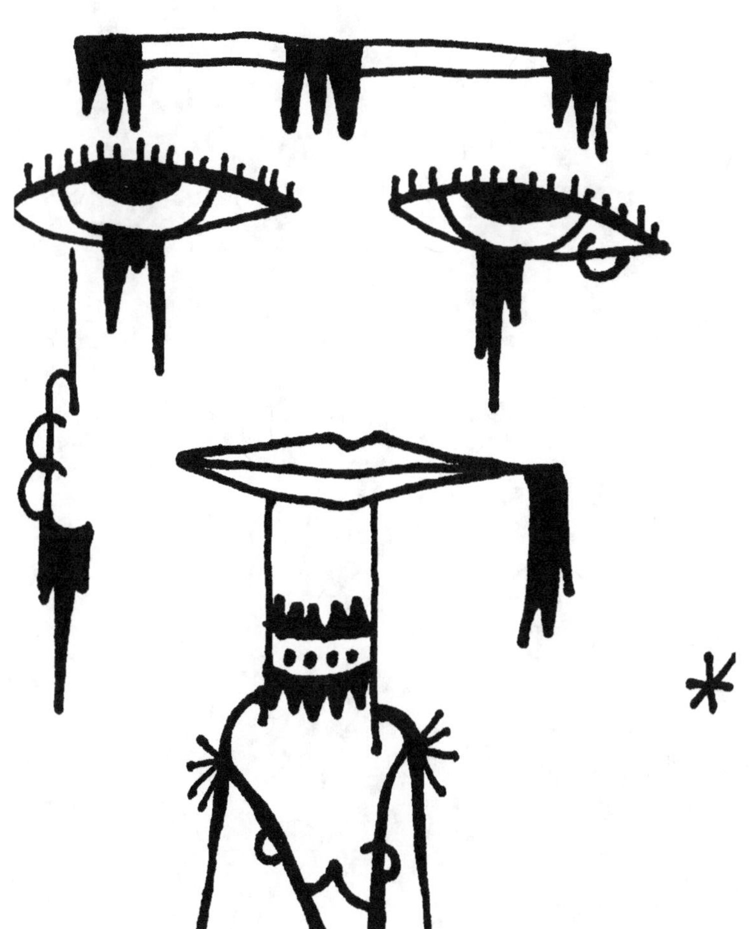

music & art

When your buddy is making an asshole of himself
playing air guitar throw him a little back up and play
air base with overbite.

If you not air talented... play air tambourine.

Big A.J.

Dude, can I play air cowbell?

Frag

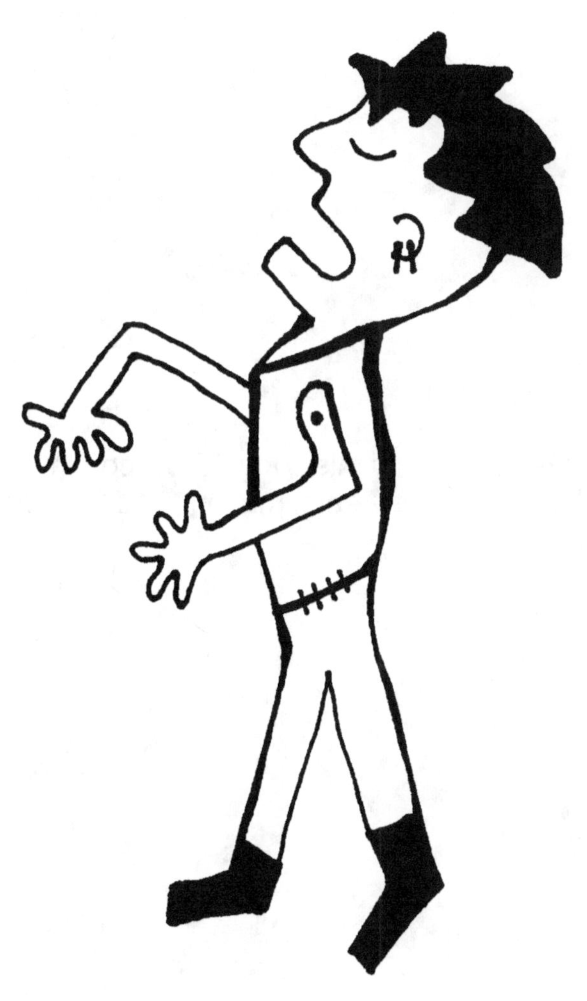

So, she was singing to this song, "Slow comin'
Walter," and Georgette said, ma, no... it's "Smoke
on the Water."

Glen the Mailman

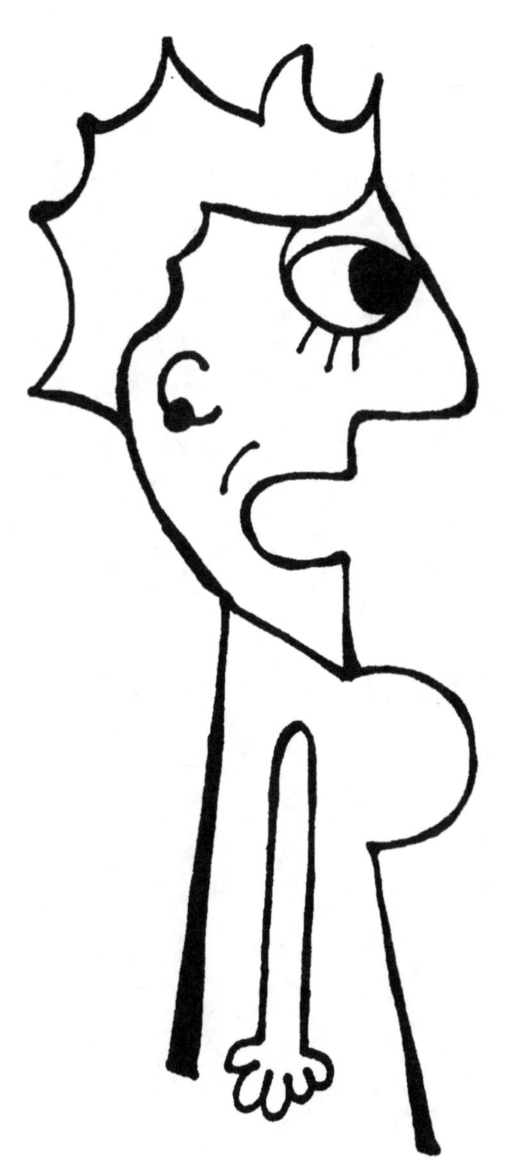

That's my album cover... one foot in the
gutter... one out.

Heavy Metal James

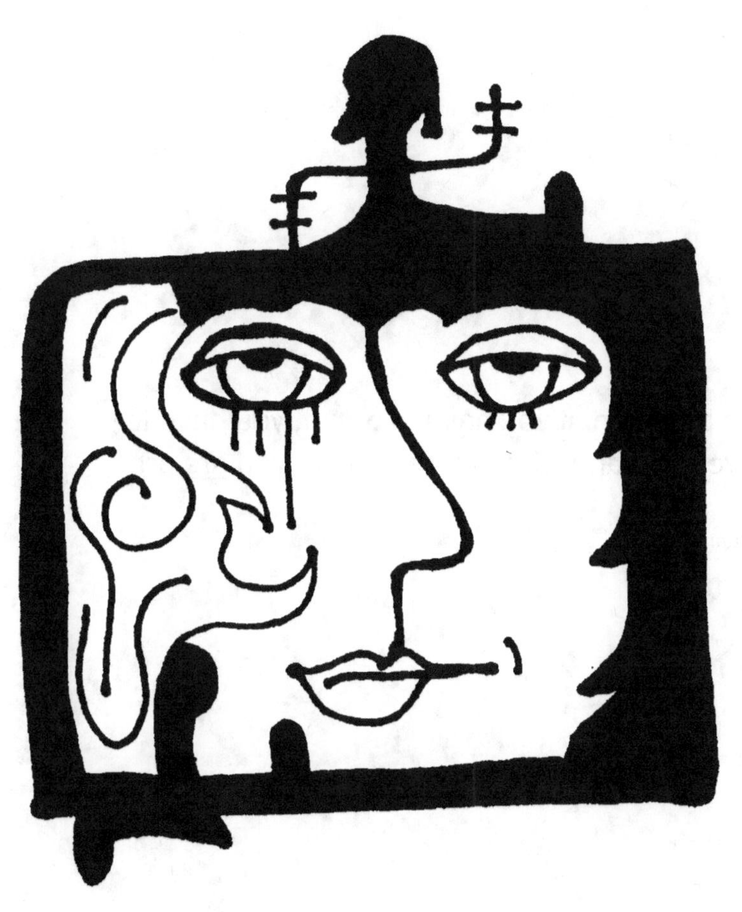

To be an artist you have to be art, you have to live art... and when you show up, you _are_ art.

Naar

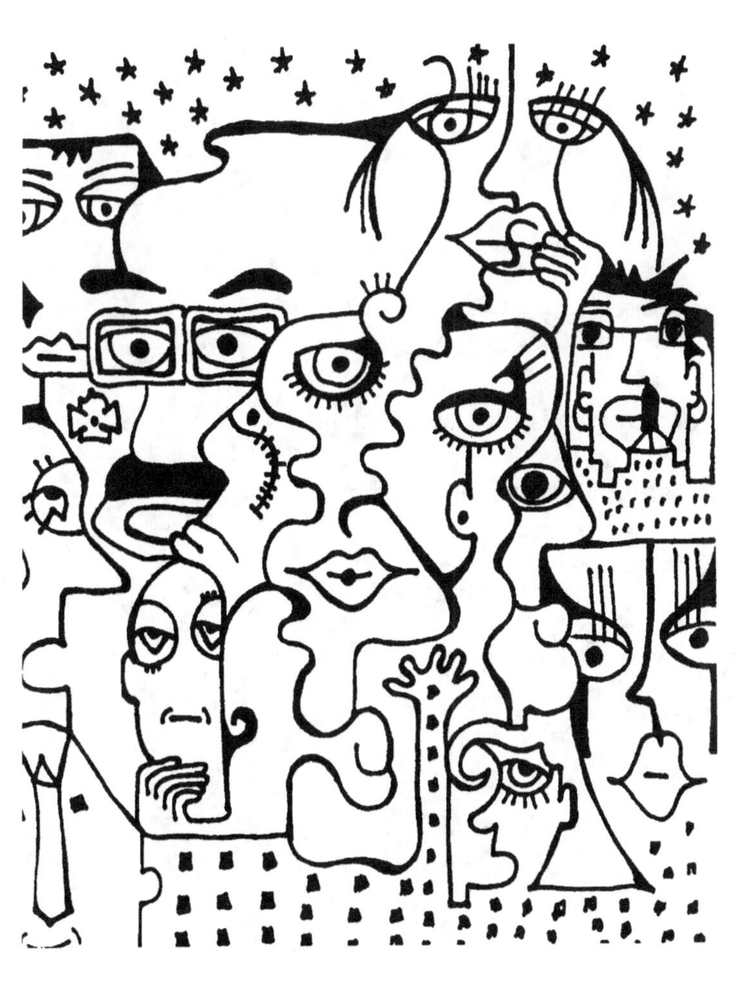

I never play good until I kill a man first.

I didn't say it like that... it was more poetic.

Mike Rock

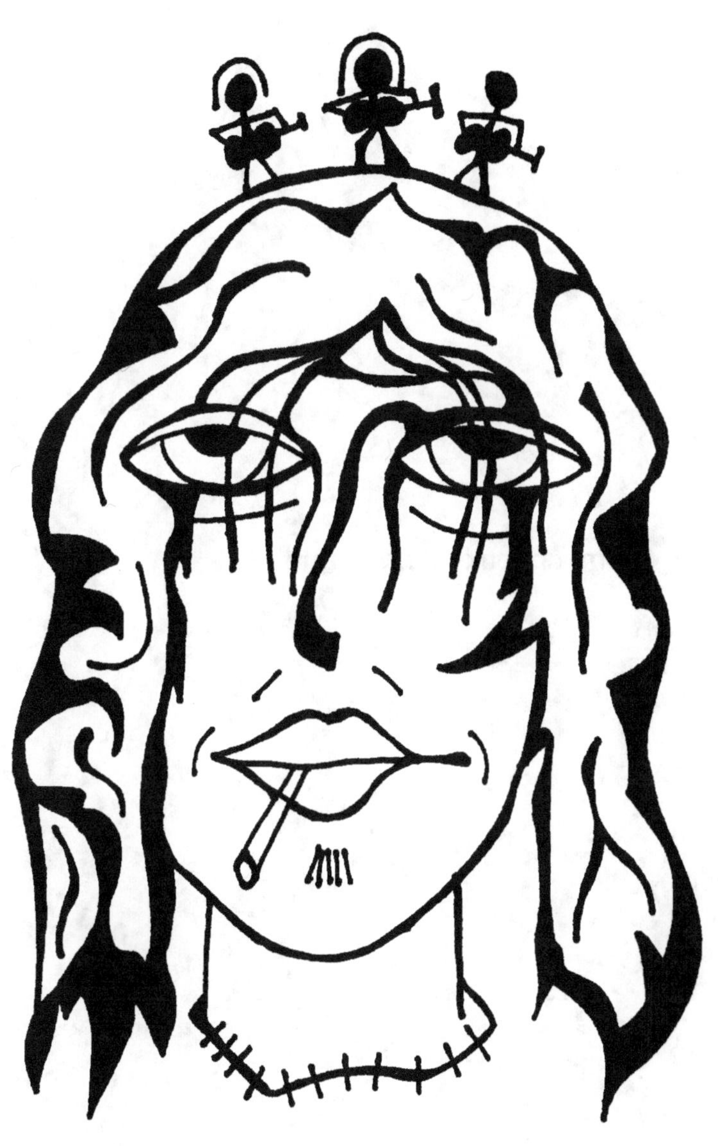

You're too much rock for one hand.

Tim the Grip

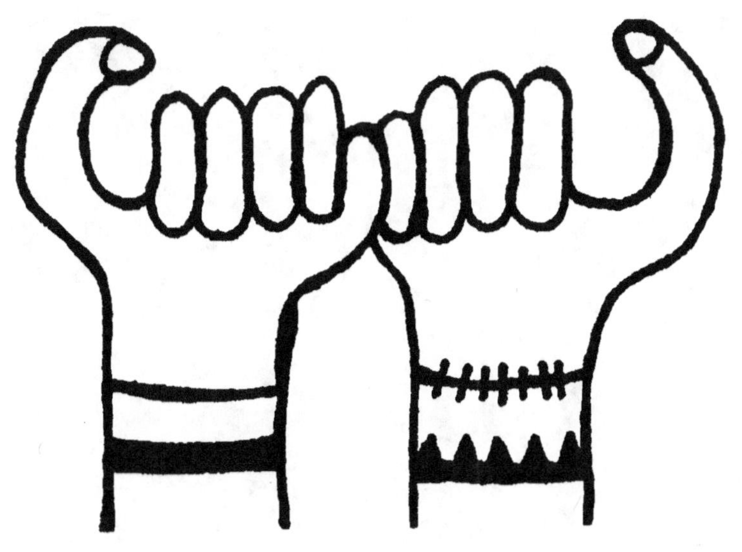

words of wisdom

Leadership is the habit of making others successful.

Young Keith

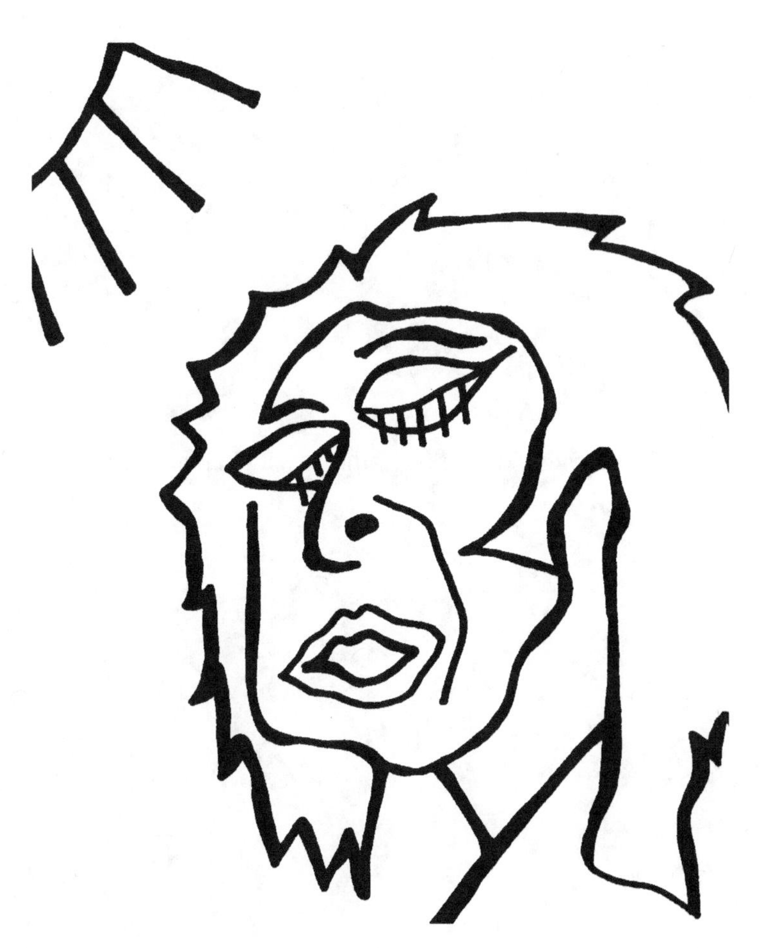

If you can't fix it with a beer or a hammer... it ain't fixable.

Anonymous

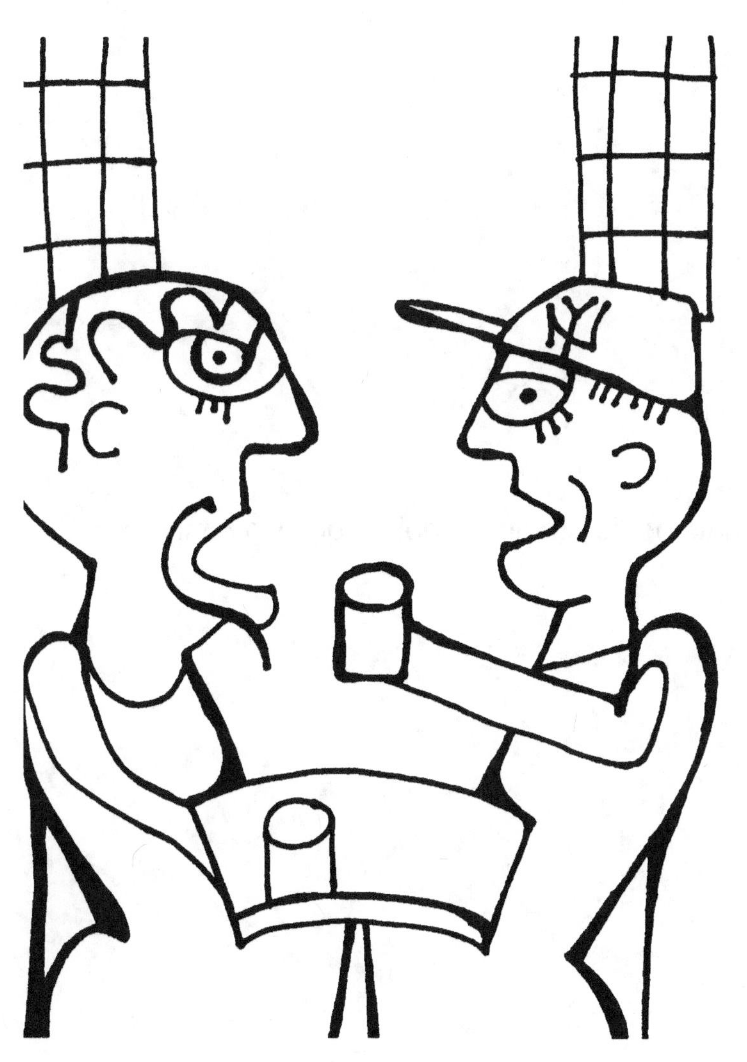

That door is like an asshole... one way only.

MCJ

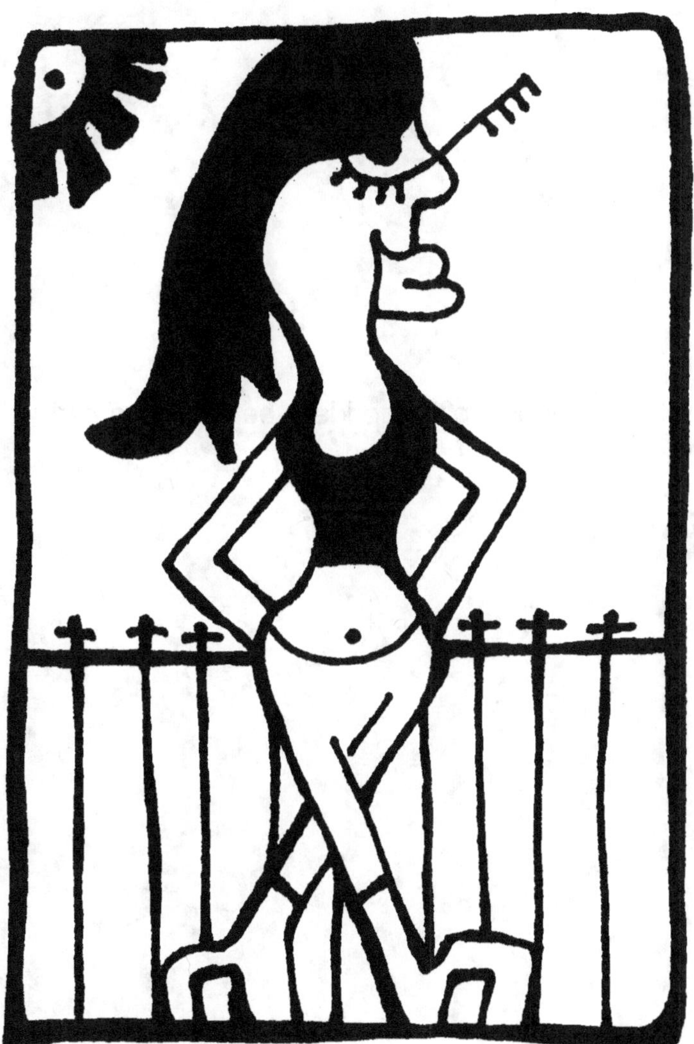

EXIT

You've got to worship the goddess before you enter
the temple.

Mary

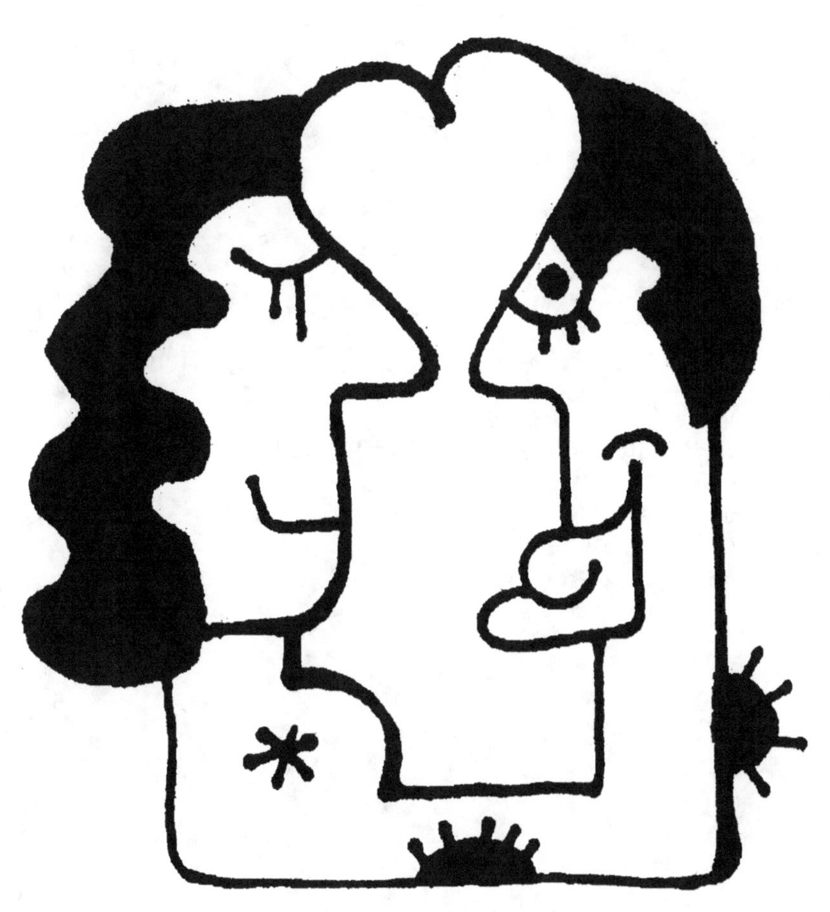

One man's junkie is another man's fortune.

Anonymous

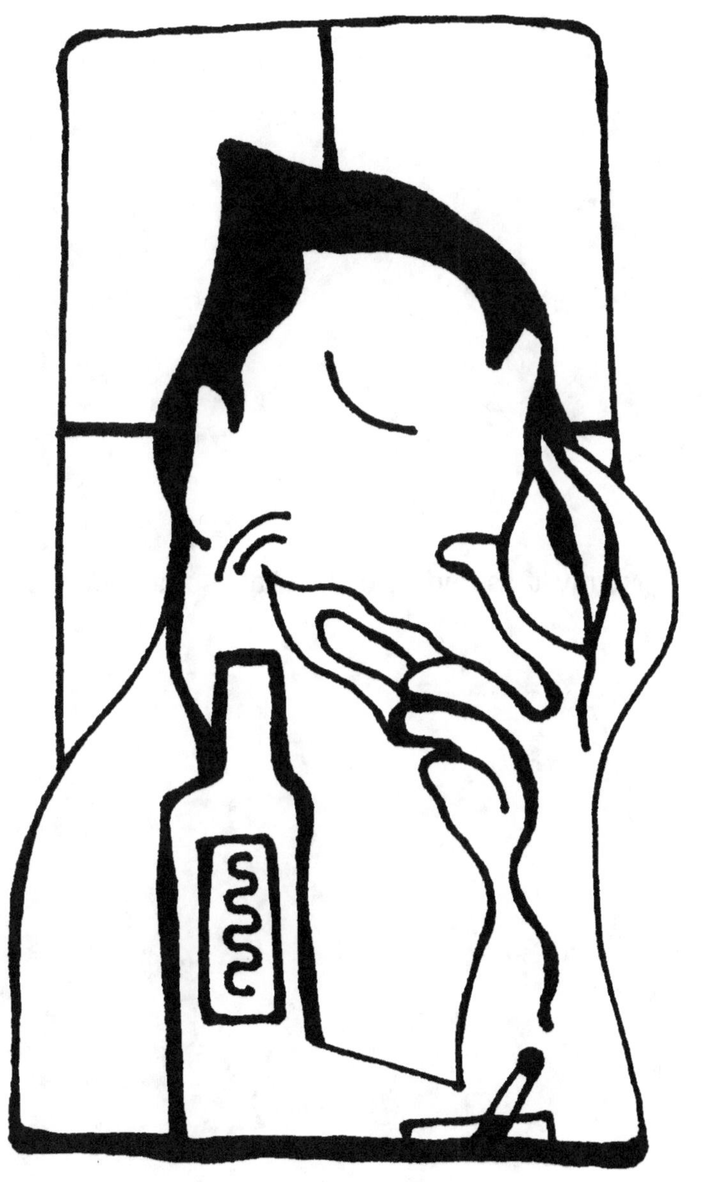

I don't like my life summed up in a little sentence.

M.R.

Special Thanks to:

Edgard Moscatelli, for the design of the book

Bryan Thatcher, for the book production
bryanthatcher.com

All the crazy and beautiful East Village characters that I have
had the grace to be friends with over the years.

www.ingramcontent.com/pod-product-compliance
Lightning Source LLC
Chambersburg PA
CBHW071214240726
48654CB00009B/780